The Tassajara

Bread Book

1970–
1976   18TH PRINTING
pickwick

the
Tassajara
Bread Book

by

Edward Espe Brown

1970

Shambhala • Boulder

Shambhala Publications, Inc.
1123 Spruce Street
Boulder, Colorado 80302

© 1970 by the Chief Priest, Zen Center, San Francisco

ISBN 0-87773-025-3
LCC 75-143877

Front Cover: Kent Rush
Calligraphy: Robert Steiner
Illustrations: Frances Thompson and Kent Rush
Back Cover: Lucille Harris
Typography: Beverly Anderson Graphic Design, San Francisco

First Printing October 1970
Second Printing (with revisions) February 1971
Third Printing March 1971
Fourth Printing May 1971
Fifth Printing (with additional revisions) September 1971
Sixth Printing January 1972
Seventh Printing September 1972
Eighth Printing January 1973
Ninth Printing May 1973
Tenth Printing October 1973
Eleventh Printing November 1973
Twelfth Printing February 1973
Thirteenth Printing May 1974
Fourteenth Printing August 1974
Fifteenth Printing April 1975
Sixteenth Printing August 1975
Seventeenth Printing March 1976
Eighteenth Printing October 1976

Distributed in the United States by Random House, Inc.
and in Canada by Random House of Canada Ltd.

Distributed in the Commonwealth by
Routledge & Kegan Paul Ltd.
London and Henley-on-Thames

Printed in the United States of America

DEDICATED
with respect and appreciation
to all my teachers
past, present and future:
gods, men and demons;
beings, animate and inanimate
living and dead, alive and dying.

Rock and Water
Wind and Tree
Bread Dough Rising

Vastly all
Are patient with me.

"We need more cooks,
not more cookbooks."

Charles V. W. Brooks

Bread makes itself, by your kindness, with your help, with
imagination running through you, with dough under hand,
you are breadmaking itself, which is why breadmaking
is so fulfilling and rewarding.

A recipe doesn't belong to anyone. Given to me, I give it
to you. Only a guide, only a skeletal framework. You must
fill in the flesh according to your nature and desire. Your
life, your love will bring these words into full creation. This
cannot be taught. You already know. So please cook,
love, feel, create.

TABLE OF CONTENTS

INTRODUCTION

Mix some flour with enough water to form a dough,
a touch of salt perhaps; shape it, bake it, the result is bread
in its simplest, most fundamental form:

> coarse, crusty
> with rich true-spirited flavor
> that one soon learns to love and crave.

Everything else is extra: yeast, milk, oil, sweetening,
eggs. Extra to make bread more palatable, more "civilized",
more chewable and sliceable; yet in a way the extras only
detract from the primitive simplicity of grain-tasting
unyeasted bread.

The range of breads and other bakery goods is extra-
ordinary, from the simplest flour-salt-water to the fanciest
butter-eggs-milk-yeasted pastry (see a good gourmet cookbook). Yet basically it's just you and the dough—ripening,
maturing, baking, blossoming together.

A COMPOSITE OF KITCHEN NECESSITIES

Bringing food alive with your
loving presence.
To have compassion, to have respect
for fresh foods, for broken bowls,
for dirty napkins, and little bugs.
To take care of leftovers,
not saying, oh that's all right, we have plenty
we can throw that away.
Because everything is saying love me,
have compassion, hold me gently.
Please hug me now and then
(we're really one, not two),
but don't get attached
(we're really two, not one).
The bowls and knives, the table, the teapot,
the leftovers, the molding vegetables,
the juicy fruit,
everything is asking this of you:
make full use,
take loving care
of me.
The cups, the glasses, the sponges,
the sticky honey jar,
all asking to fulfill.
Just to make deepest love all the time,
concentrating not on the food, but on yourself:
making your best effort to allow things
to fulfill their functions. In this way
everything is deliciously full
of warmth and kindness.

I never would have done this without TASSAJARA.
I have never cooked like this away from Tassajara.
Coming from the Earth, returning to the Earth,
transformed and transforming the material spirit:
I am consumed.
If you must cook,
    please offer yourself
    a substantial piece of emptiness.
    Hold back nothing,
    until you experience offering,
    "Eat me! and be nourished."
Homage to the Perfection of Wisdom,
    the Infinite, the Holy:
everything is leading you, pushing you,
instructing you, bugging you to supreme,
perfect enlightenment. This means
there are no mistakes. You might do it
differently next time, but that's because
you did it this way this time.
Perfect, even if you say
too much this too little that.
It's you and please be yourself.
Offer yourself.
Feels good. O.K.?
Cooking is not simply in the tongue,
in the palate.
It is in the whole body
flowing out of the groin and chest
through arms and hands.

INGREDIENTS

*"Love is not only the most important ingredient:
it is the only ingredient which really matters."*

—from a cookbook by a British chef

The ingredients listed are mostly "whole" foods. This "wholeness" means that the flour, meal (a coarser grind than flour), or flakes contain all the elements of the whole grain, particularly the "germ", that part of the grain kernel from which the grain would sprout if planted. So this germ is the most life-containing, life-giving part of the grain. Studies show this in terms of its being higher in vitamins and essential oils than other parts of the grain.

For this reason "whole" corn meal, which contains the germ, will have a greater life-containing, life-giving quality than the "degermed" cornmeal found in supermarkets. Whole cornmeal is a "live" food—it spoils when the oil in the germ becomes rancid. Degermed cornmeal is a "dead" food, as it lacks the germ (of life). Hence, it can be kept on grocery shelves for months without spoiling, though like all milled grains it does become stale.

In any case, best to buy grain products as freshly-milled as possible, and to preserve their freshness by refrigerating in sealed jars or plastic bags. Information on where to purchase whole grain products is at the end of this section on ingredients. But don't let a lack of whole grain products keep you from making bread. Most of the recipes can be made with regular white flour, if necessary.

Whole wheat flour:

provides the basic foundation of bread. With a deep, full-flavored, hearty, wheat taste, it contains all the elements of the wheat kernel: flour, bran and germ. The bran and germ have good amounts of B vitamins. Stoneground whole wheat flour has a fresher taste and higher nutritional properties than flour produced from high-speed milling, due to the lower temperatures of stone grinding. Wheat flour contains the highest amount of "gluten", a substance which holds air in the dough and expands like hundreds of small balloons, giving dough its elasticity. For this reason most of the bread recipes include at least one-half whole wheat or unbleached white flour.

Unbleached white flour:

is mechanically refined to remove the bran and germ, has not been chemically treated and contains no preserving chemicals. Compared with the standard all-purpose bleached white flours, it has a distinctly "live" taste. The high gluten content of white flour makes it particularly useful in breadmaking. Small amounts of this flour (10%) give lightness and increased workability to bread doughs. If bread dough is too heavy or too sticky, add more white flour next time. Use also for special occasions and particular recipes which are of a lighter and more delicate nature.

Rye flour:

contains a lesser amount of gluten than wheat, and tends to produce a fine-textured, moist, dense bread. Small amounts (10–15%) add smoothness and workability to doughs with a high proportion of granular ingredients, e.g. corn-rye, rye-oatmeal. Large amounts of rye flour tend to produce a sticky dough.

Corn meal:

gives breads a more crumbly texture, a crunchiness and sweetness. *Whole* corn meal, though it spoils more readily, is superior in taste and nutriment to the degermed corn meal found in supermarkets. Meal is a coarser grind than flour.

Millet\meal:

though somewhat bland-tasting, adds a surprising crunchy richness to breads.

Rolled oats:

make bread chewy, moist, sweet. Their white flakes often make a beautiful mosaic in molasses-darkened breads. For rolled oats as distinct from oatmeal, whole oat kernels are pressed flat between rollers. Oatmeal has most often been subjected to a greater amount of processing. Oats are the grain richest in minerals, salt, fat, and protein.

Barley flour:

is particularly delicious in breads if pan-toasted before being added to the bread dough. As such it gives breads a sweet, moist, cake-like quality.

Brown rice flour:

is sweet and will tend to make bread moist, dense, and smooth. Cooked brown rice gives bread a moist, chewy character.

Buckwheat flour:

has a very distinctive taste and will tend to make bread heavy and "full" of warmth.

8

Whole grains and cracked grains:

should be cooked before being added to bread. If using cooked grains, less water or more flour will be necessary.

Yeast:

is a microscopic fungus, which as a by-product of its existence, makes bread rise. All yeasted recipes use dry baker's yeast.

Milk:

makes bread smoother, softer, more cake-like, and modifies, masks the "coarse" grain taste. Recipes call for dry milk, though whole milk can be used if scalded (heated to just below boiling) and then cooled to lukewarm. This has to do with killing various enzymes which would otherwise interfere with the activity of the yeast.

Eggs:

will make bread lighter, more airy, tender and give a golden color.

Oil:

makes a richer-tasting, cakier bread. Non-hydrogenated liquid vegetable oils are more readily digested and usefully assimilated by the body than hydrogenated (solidified or hardened) oils such as shortening and margarine, though the use of these hardened oils tends to make a flakier dough.

"Cold pressed" oils are likely to be higher in essential fatty acids than regular commercial oils. Even so, most cold pressed oils are highly refined, so that they are clear, light, and nearly colorless. Oils in their more raw state are cloudy, and tend to smell strongly of the plant of derivation. Also they are more *oily*.

Once again it is a question of commercial value as opposed to human welfare. Those oils which are more highly refined and processed will keep better (often with the use of preservatives) and are "purer", so they are more practical for shipping, storing, and selling to a public, which generally prefers the cheaper, "sanitized" product.

A corn germ oil (distributed by Erewhon), available in some health food stores, is quite delicious (it can be used in place of butter or margarine) as well as being high in essential fatty acids and natural anti-oxidants (rancidity-retarders normally processed out of the oil).

Sweetenings:

tend to stimulate the appetite (more, more). Honey or molasses are used in most recipes calling for sweetening, though in some cases their use is impractical. "Unfiltered, unblended, uncooked" honey will contain more enzymes and minerals than regular commercial honey. Molasses, particularly blackstrap molasses, contains valuable amounts of B vitamins and minerals, including iron. Blackstrap does have a distinctive, strong taste. Honey or molasses will make the bread pleasantly fragrant as well as sweet. Sugar, particularly white sugar, has a noted lack of any nutritive factors aside from calories. This tends to create an over-abundance of sugar in the body, eventually resulting in lowered blood sugar or less energy.

Dates or raisins or other dried fruits may also replace some of the sweetening.

Salt:

will give its unique benefits. Sea salt or unrefined salt contains numerous trace elements often lacking in the usual diet.

Carob flour:
is used in some of the recipes. Carob has a naturally
sweet taste similar to chocolate. It is a very wholesome,
well-balanced, readily digestible food containing good
amounts of B vitamins, vitamin A, minerals, and protein,
as opposed to chocolate which is not noted as a balanced
food, capable of being a dietary staple. For special occasions,
however, chocolate does provide a noticeable "hit"
unobtainable from carob.

WHERE TO BUY

Where oh where. It is necessary to have some ingredients
before you can begin cooking. Often this is the most difficult
part of providing food for people, particularly since natural,
whole foods are strikingly unavailable and/or outrageously
expensive at most supermarkets. For example, try finding
unbleached white flour or corn meal which has not been "degermed". (There's going to be a revolution.) Health food
stores are something of a source, though here too the emphasis
tends to be on packaged, processed foods.

If no health food stores are available in your area, you
may buy stoneground flour from:

El Molino Mills, P.O. Box 2025, Alhambra, California 91803
Walnut Acres, Penn's Creek, Pennsylvania 17862
Great Valley Mills, Quakertown, Bucks County, Pennsylvania 18951
The Vermont Country Store, Weston, Vermont 05161
Spiral Foods, Inc., 1017 Willow Street, Chico, California 95926
Arrowhead Mills, Inc., P.O.Box 866, Hereford, Texas 79045
Ted A. Whitmer & Son, Bloomfield, Montana 59315
Erewhon Trading Co., 8003 Beverly Blvd., Los Angeles, Calif. 90048
Erewhon Trading Co., 33 Farnsworth Street, Boston, Mass. 02210
The Food Mill, 3033 MacArthur Blvd., Oakland, Calif. 94602

UTENSILS

TO BEGIN WITH:

Certain items will assist you in making bread, though few of them are strictly necessary. *Heavy, brown, ceramic bread bowls* are available. These hold and distribute heat well. Pre-heating the bowl allows the baby bread dough to feel at home and warmly held. A *stainless steel bread bowl* won't break. Large pots, clean buckets, or a plastic basin can provide a home for your doughs. *Mixing spoons, wood or metal, a set of measuring spoons, a 1-cup* and a *2-cup measure* are useful, along with a *rubber spatula* for cleaning cups and bowls. But, if necessary, you *can* do all the measuring and mixing with your hands. Most of the recipes are approximations anyway to give you *some* idea. Learn to feel for yourself, through experience and experimentation.

A *good-sized bread board* for kneading is something worth taking good care of. Use it only for breads. Don't cut on it, and store it in a clean, dry place. Keep it clean and dry. A wet towel between the board and the table will keep it from slipping. Kneading right on the table is all right, too, if you keep it carefully cleaned. A table approximately at the height at which your hands rest comfortably allows ease in kneading. Give yourself plenty of clear open space to work in.

Bread pans, sometimes aluminum and rectangular; 5¼ x 9¼ or 4½ x 8½ are standard sizes. For small loaves, use pans 3¾ x 7½. Don't wash them but once a year, and they will develop dark tempering. The bread will bake faster and not stick. Other possibilities include *cookie sheets, metal cups, glass or enamel pans, small ceramic flower pots;*

let their shape be the shape of your breads. An *oven for baking,* although you can always make any bread into English muffins, or crackers, if you have a griddle, or a frying pan, and stove or fire.

ABOUT YEAST

Waiting-on-yeast is to feed, keep house, keep it warm, clean its air, empty its garbage, and cater to its whims. Getting angry at its failings does not help. To provide patient loving care and food for growth does. Begin by dissolving the dry yeast in lukewarm water 90 to 105° F. At temperatures much higher than 105°, the yeast becomes very frantically active and soon exhausts itself; at lower temperatures it lives a more dormant existence, until below freezing, it barely respirates.

Most bread recipes say, "dissolve the yeast in ¼ cup lukewarm water. Scald milk . . ." This method does of course produce excellent results (and we include some of those recipes); however, it is sufficient and timely to dissolve the yeast in the entire amount of water and then stir in the powdered milk, in which case as is noticeable, the milk need not be scalded.

Yeast needs oxygen to breathe and simple sugars to eat. Though some simple sugars are present in flour, due to action of enzymes on complexer starch molecules, generally some sweetening is added for the yeast to dine on. Treat it to molasses: mild or a little blackstrap; honey: avocado, buckwheat, tupolo, or choice fancy; brown or white sugars; corn syrup. Living yeast turns the oxygen and sugars into carbon dioxide and alcohols. (Brewers' yeast is an even better alcohol producer.) The carbon dioxide becoming trapped in the glutenous network of dough is what makes the bread rise.

Take care that the carbon dioxide and the alcohols do not build up extensively enough that the yeast suffocates and generally expires in its own wastes. Punching down the

14

dough or otherwise working with it releases gaseous
by-products of the yeast existence and freshens its air.
Bake the bread, and the yeast dies. Slice it, butter it,
eat it. Be thankful.

General Directions

for

Tassajara Basic

Yeasted Bread

GENERAL DIRECTIONS FOR
TASSAJARA BASIC YEASTED BREAD

I. Mixing up the Sponge
   Setting the Dough to Rise
   Advantages of Sponge Method

II. Folding in Oil, Salt, and Dry Ingredients
   Kneading the Dough
   Rising and Punching the Dough
   Shaping the Loaves
   Pre-Baking and Baking
   Storing

Yeasted breads tend to be sweet and rich-tasting due to the use of milk, eggs, oil, honey, molasses.

Made principally with wheat flour, bread can also incorporate a wide variety of other whole grains to give varying textures and tastes. As described in the section on INGREDIENTS, rye, corn, millet, barley, rice, oats and buckwheat may be used. For further variation and nutriment one may add soy sauce, sesame seeds, cheese, nuts or dried fruit. Once the dough is ready for baking, there are many ways to shape and bake it. The Tassajara Yeasted Bread Recipe leads into all the other yeasted bread and pastry recipes: rye-oatmeal, corn-rye, English muffins and cinnamon rolls, etc.

I(A)   MIXING UP THE SPONGE

(Four loaves; all measurements are for Basic Tassajara
Yeasted Bread Recipe No. 1.)

6 c lukewarm water (85—105°)
2 T yeast (2 packages)
½—¾ c sweetening (honey, molasses or brown sugar)
2 c dry milk (optional)
7—9 c whole wheat flour (substitute 2 or more cups
unbleached white flour if desired)

Measure the WATER (6 cups); lukewarm (85—105°), does
not feel warm or cold on your wrist.

Measure the dry BAKER'S YEAST (2 T); for faster rising
and lighter bread, use 1½—2 times amount in recipe.

Sprinkle YEAST over water and stir lightly to dissolve.

Add SWEETENING (½—¾ cup); rinse measuring cup in
liquid to clean. ¾ cup sweetening for four loaves will
make a "sweet" dough. ¼ cup sweetening would be
quite sufficient for the growth of the yeast, while
larger amounts may be added for sweet tooths.

Add DRY MILK and stir to dissolve. Complete dissolving
is not necessary (Figure 1), as the ingredients will
become well mixed when the batter is thicker. The
bread will have a grainier taste and a coarser texture
if the dry milk is omitted. In this case less flour will
be needed.

If EGGS are desired, beat and add at this stage, adding more
flour if needed for proper consistency of dough. Or
eggs may be added to the completed sponge *after* flour
is in and the batter beaten. Let the sponge rise 10—15
minutes while you separate the eggs and beat the yolks

20

1

2

3

4

5

6

21

and whites. First fold in beaten yolks, and then the
stiffly beaten whites. Let rise an additional 30—40
minutes before continuing.

Then add WHOLE WHEAT FLOUR a cup or so at a time,
stirring briskly after each addition (Figure 2). As
mixture thickens, begin beating with the spoon,
stirring up and down in small strokes and in small
circles at the surface of the mixture (Figures 4 and 5).
Scrape sides of bowl occasionally (Figure 3). After
7—8 cups of flour have been added, the mixture will
be quite thick, but still beatable, a thick mud.

Now BEAT about 100 TIMES (Figures 4 and 5) until the
batter is very smooth. Do this at the surface of the dough,
ducking the spoon under the surface, bringing it up
above the surface pulling up the batter in a circular
motion. The dough will become stretchier as you do
this and much air will be incorporated.

This completes the mixing of the sponge.

(B) SETTING THE DOUGH TO RISE

COVER the bowl with a damp towel to keep off draft
(Figure 6). Set in warmish place (about 85—100°).
In summer almost any place might do. Otherwise
on top of stove over pilot light, shelf above hot water
heater, in oven which has pilot light, or in oven which
has been on low heat (250—300°) for five to ten
minutes. Whichever. If it's in a cooler place (70—85°)
it'll just rise more slowly. If it's frozen it won't rise at
all but will rise when it's unfrozen. Heat above about
125—130° will kill yeast, which is what happens when
the bread is baked.

Let it RISE for an hour or 45 or 70 minutes.

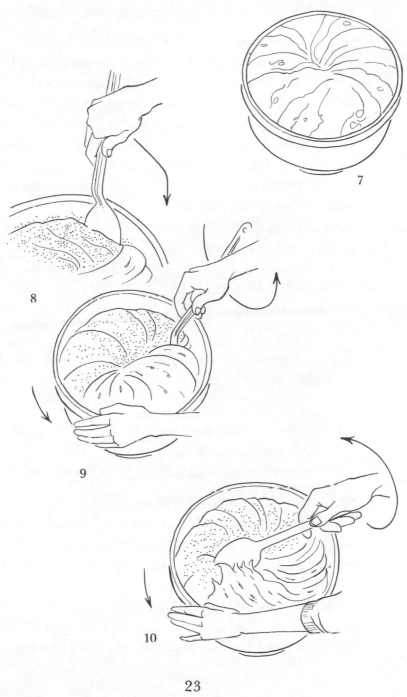

7

8

9

10

23

(C) ADVANTAGES OF SPONGE METHOD

The sponge method, omitted in most bread recipes, is
advantageous in many ways. The yeast gets started
easily in the absence of salt, which inhibits its func-
tioning, and in the presence of plenty of oxygen.
Gluten is formed when the sponge stretches in rising,
which would otherwise be the product of *your* labor
in kneading. This added elasticity makes the remaining
ingredients more easily incorporated and kneading
more easily accomplished. Even a 10—15 minute
rising at this point will facilitate the accomplishment
of the remaining steps.

II(A) FOLDING IN OIL, SALT AND DRY INGREDIENTS (OTHER FLOURS, NUTS, FRUITS, ETC.)

(Four loaves; all measurements are for Basic Tassajara
Yeasted Bread Recipe No. 1.)

2½ T salt
½ c oil (or butter, margarine, etc.)
6—8 c whole wheat flour
2—3 c additional whole wheat flour for kneading

FOLDING IN is the method used to mix from this point on
(Figure 7). DO NOT STIR. Do not cut through the
dough. Keep it in one piece as much as possible. Each
cut and tear will lessen the elasticity and strength of
the dough.
Pour on OIL and sprinkle in SALT. Stir around *side* of bowl
(Figure 8) and fold over toward center (Figures 9 and
10). Turn bowl toward you with left hand and repeat

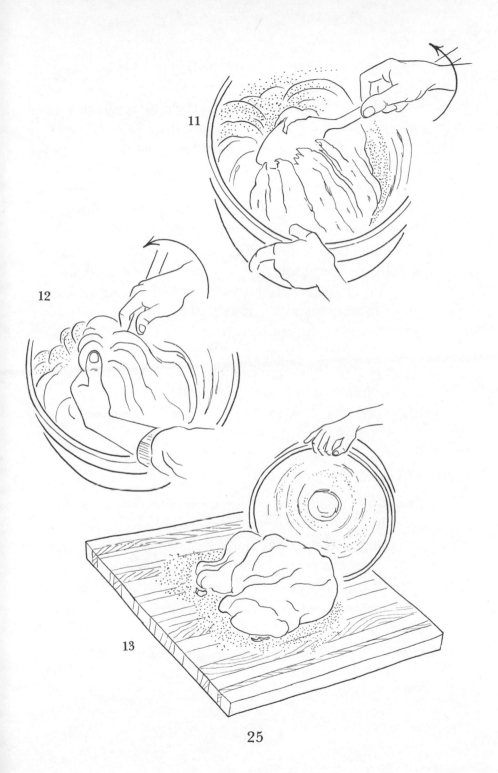

11

12

13

25

folding until oil and salt are incorporated (Figures
    8, 9, 10).

Sprinkle DRY INGREDIENTS on surface of dough about
    a cup at a time. Fold wet mixture from sides of bowl
    on top of dry ingredients. Turn the bowl ¼ turn between
    folds (Figures 8, 9, 10). When dry ingredients are
    moistened by the dough, add some more dry ingredients
    (Figures 11 and 12). Continue folding. After adding
    6—8 cups of wheat flour, the dough will become very
    thick and heavy, but don't be intimidated. Continue
    folding in flour until dough comes away from (does
    not stick to) sides and bottom of bowl, sitting up in
    bowl in a big lump (Figure 12). The dough is ready for
    kneading when it can be turned out of bowl in pretty
    much of a piece, except for a few remaining scraps
    (Figure 13). Take time to scrape bowl carefully, and
    lay scrapings on top of dough on floured board. It is
    not necessary to wash the bread bowl at this point,
    simply oil it lightly.

(B) KNEADING THE DOUGH

The kneading surface, board or table should be at a height
    on which your hands rest comfortably when you are
    standing straight (mid-thigh). Keep the surface floured
    sufficiently to prevent the dough from sticking during
    kneading. The purpose of kneading is to get the dough
    well-mixed, of a smooth, even texture, and to further
    develop the elasticity of the dough.

Beginning with a lump of dough not entirely of a piece,
    somewhat ragged and limply-lying, commence kneading.

Flour your hands.

26

14

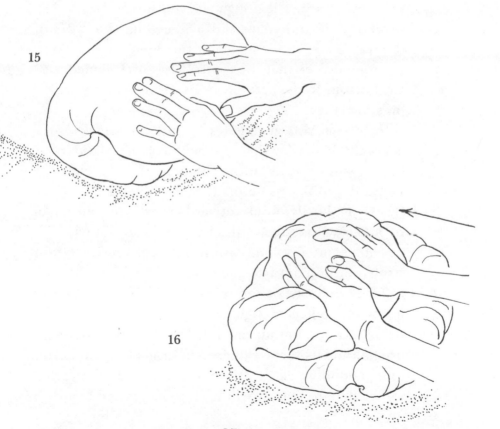

15

16

27

Picking up far edge of dough, FOLD dough IN HALF
toward you, far side over near side (Figure 14), so
that the two edges are approximately lined up evenly.

Place your hands on NEAR SIDE of dough so that the top
of your palms (just below fingers) are at the top front
of the dough (Figure 15).

PUSH DOWN AND FORWARD, centering the pushing
through the heels of the hands more and more as the
push continues (Figure 16). Relax your fingers at the
end of the push. Rock forward with your whole body
rather than simply pushing with your arms. Apply
steady, even pressure, allowing the dough to give way
at its own pace. The dough will roll forward with the
seam on top, and your hands will end up about 2/3 of
the way toward the far side of the dough. Removing
your hands, see that the top fold has been joined to
the bottom fold where the heels of the hands were
pressing (Figure 17).

TURN the dough ¼ turn (Figures 16 and 17) (clockwise
is usually easier for right-handed persons). Fold in
half towards you as before (Figure 17) and rock
forward, pushing as before (Figures 18 and 19).

TURN, FOLD, PUSH. Rock forward. Twist and fold as you
rock back. Rock forward. Little by little you will
develop some rhythm. Push firmly, yet gently, so you
stretch but do not tear the dough.

Add FLOUR to board or sprinkle on top of dough as
necessary to keep dough from sticking to board or
hands. As you knead, the dough will begin stiffening
up, holding its shape rather than sagging; it will become
more and more elastic, so that it will tend to stretch
rather than to tear. It will stick to hands and board

28

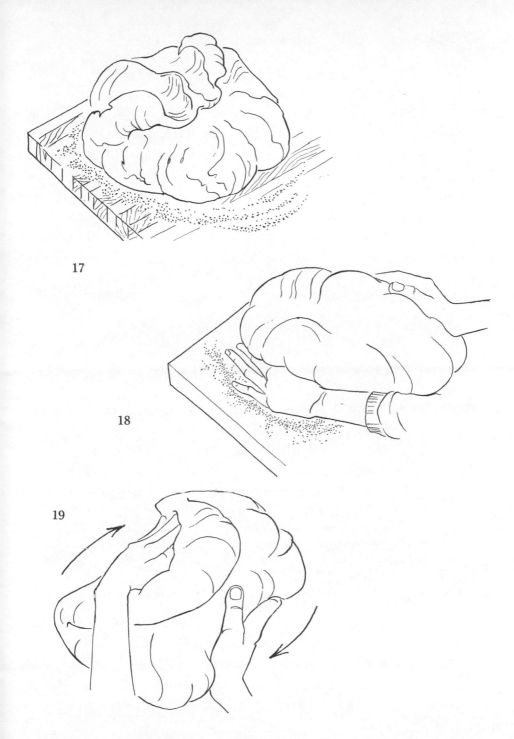

17

18

19

less and less until no flour is necessary to prevent sticking. The surface will be smooth and somewhat shiny.

Before you finish kneading, SCRAPE THE BREAD BOARD (Figure 20) and rub dough off hands and incorporate these scraps into the dough.

Place the dough (Figure 21) in the OILED BREAD BOWL smooth side down, and then turn it over so the creases are on the bottom (Figure 22). Oiled surface will keep a crust from forming on the dough.

COVER the dough with a DAMP TOWEL and set it in a warm place.

(C) RISING AND PUNCHING THE DOUGH

Let dough RISE 50—60 minutes, until nearly doubled in size (Figure 23).

"PUNCH DOWN" by pushing fist into dough, as far as the hand will go, steadily and firmly. Do this maybe 25 or 30 times all over the dough (Figure 24). It will not punch down as small as it was before rising. Cover.

Let RISE 40—50 minutes, until nearly doubled in size. If you are short for time, the second rising may be omitted. The loaves will be slightly heavier.

(D) SHAPING THE LOAVES

Start the oven pre-heating. Turn dough onto board. (Figure 25). If the dough is of proper consistency moisture-wise, no flour will be necessary on the board. If too wet it will stick on the board. Use flour as necessary. If too dry the folds will not seal together easily.

Shape into BALL by folding dough to center all the way

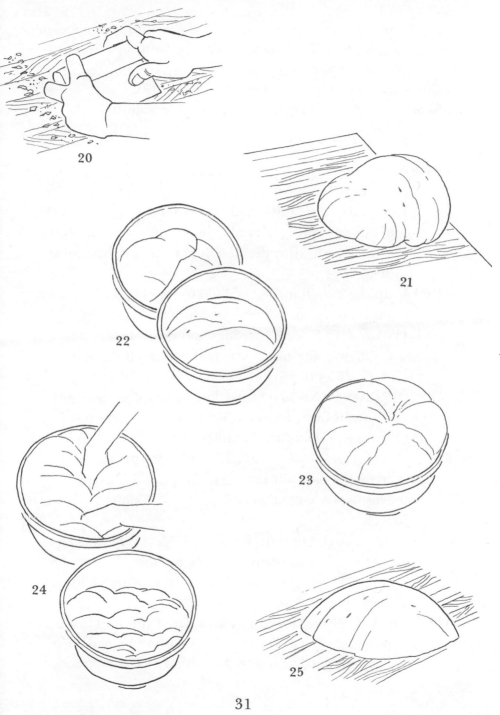

20

21

22

23

24

25

31

around (Figure 26) as in kneading without the pushing (Figure 27). Turn smooth side up, and tuck in dough all the way around (Figure 28).

Cut into FOUR EVEN PIECES (Figure 29).

Shape into BALLS again, and let sit five minutes.

TO SHAPE INTO LOAVES:

KNEAD DOUGH with right hand (Figure 30). Turn and fold dough with left hand (Figure 31). Do this about five or six times until dough is compact. This gives the loaf added "spring", similar to winding a clock. After the final push, turn the dough ¼ turn and, beginning at near edge,

ROLL up the dough into a LOG-SHAPE (Figure 32). With seam on bottom, flatten out top with finger-tips (Figure 33). Square off sides and ends (Figure 34). Turn it over and pinch seams together all the way along it (Figure 35).

Have BREAD PANS in a stack. Put some oil in top one and turn it over, letting it drain into the next one (Figure 36). Place loaf in oiled pan with seam up. Dough can fill pan one-half to two-thirds full. A 5¼ x 9¼ pan will take 2¼—2½ pound yeasted loaves. A 4½ x 8½ pan will take 1¾—2 pound yeasted loaves.

FLATTEN dough out with backs of fingers (Figure 37). Turn loaf over so seam is on the bottom (Figures 38 and 39). Press again into shape of pan with backs of fingers (Figure 37).

COVER. Let RISE 15—25 minutes, from finish of last loaf, depending partly on how long you take to make the loaves and partly on how fast the dough is rising.

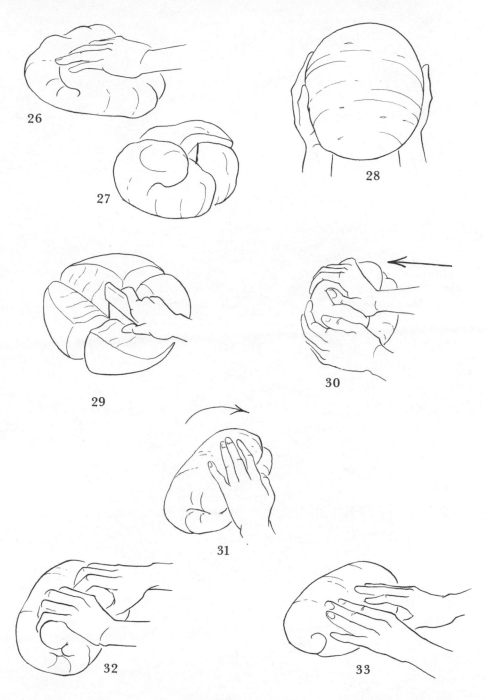

26

27

28

29

30

31

32

33

33

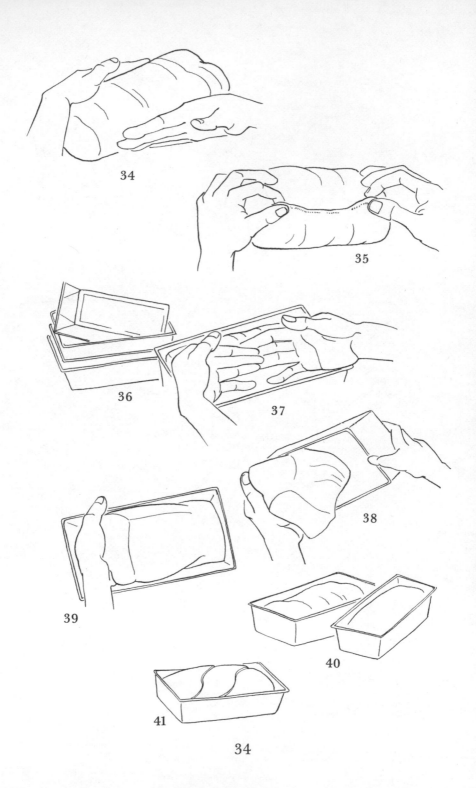

34
35
36
37
38
39
40
41

34

Center of loaf will be up level with top of pan by this
time (Figure 40).

(E) PRE-BAKING AND BAKING

Cut the top with SLITS ½ inch deep to allow steam to
escape (Figure 41). For golden brown, shiny surface,
Brush SURFACE of loaf with EGG WASH: one egg beaten
with ¼ to ½ cup water or milk.
Sprinkle with SESAME SEED or POPPY SEED, if you wish.
BAKE at 350° for 50—70 minutes. (Smaller loaves will bake
faster.) To see if done: top is shiny golden brown. The
sides and bottoms should likewise be golden brown.
Loaf will resound with deep hollow thump when
tapped with finger.
REMOVE from pans immediately.
For clean-cut slices, LET COOL one hour or more before
cutting.
Note: Adjustment of oven temperature may be necessary.
Electric ovens, especially, should probably be set 25°
lower than indicated temperature.

(F) STORING

When completely cooled, bread may be kept in a sealed
plastic bag in the refrigerator. Finished bread may
also be frozen and thawed for later use, with some
impairment of flavor and freshness. Slightly stale bread
may be freshened by heating in 350° oven for 10—15
minutes. Dry bread can still be used for toast or French
toast, croutons or breadcrumbs.
For zweiback, cut dry bread in cubes and rebake at 200°
until crunchy and dry.

ROLLS AND OTHER SHAPES

Though they are usually made with a bread dough rich with butter and eggs, rolls can actually be made from any bread dough. If short for time before a meal, rolls have the advantage of baking faster than bread, and being servable immediately out of the oven, while bread must cool before it can be well-sliced.

Figure 12—15 rolls per loaf of bread dough.

GENERAL DIRECTIONS FOR ROLLS

Form into a LOG SHAPE about one loaf's worth of bread dough; log should be 1½—2" diameter (Figure 42) and is formed by rolling dough between hands and bread board.

SECTION log into equal-sized pieces (Figure 43).

SHAPE into one or more of the following types of rolls or some other shape.

Let RISE 20 minutes.

EGG WASH.

(Sprinkle with poppy or sesame seed.)

BAKE about 25 minutes at 375° until nicely browned.

Plain Rolls (the simplest, plainest)
Place the sectioned pieces on edge or flat on a greased sheet or a sheet sprinkled with corn meal. (Figure 44)

Clover Leaf Rolls
Divide sections into three pieces. Shape each into a ball. Place three balls in greased muffin cup. (Figures 45 and 49)

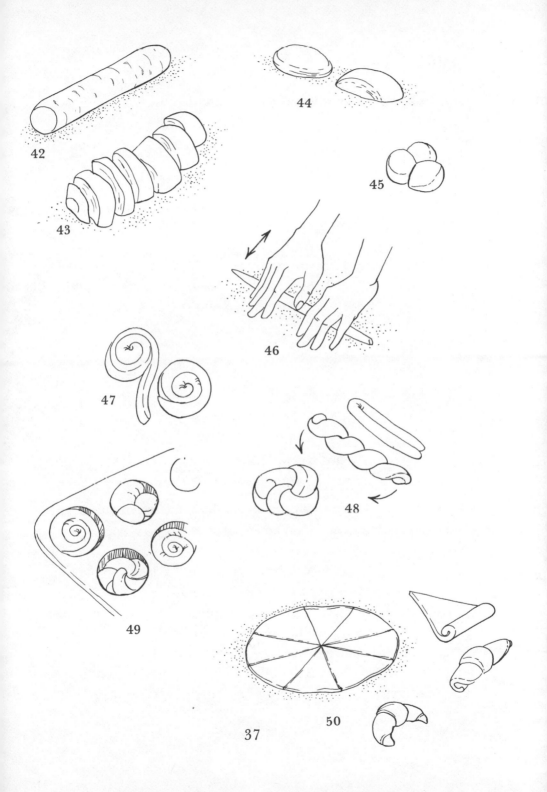

42

43

44

45

46

47

48

49

50

37

Snail or Spiral Rolls

Roll each section into a length about 6" long. Coil it
up and place in greased muffin cup. (Figures 46, 47, 49)

Flower Rolls

Roll each section into a length 8" long. Fold double,
end to end, and twist. Then coil and place in greased
muffin cup. (Figures 48 and 49)

Butterhorn or Crescent

Do not shape dough into log. Roll out in a circle about
¼ inch thick. Brush with melted butter or margarine.
Cut in 8–12 wedges. Roll up starting from wide end.
Twist to form crescent. Place on greased sheet.
(Figure 50)

FRUIT-FILLED LOAVES

Any yeasted bread dough can be made into fruit-filled
loaves braided on top. Make any size loaf.

FLATTEN dough into a rectangle about ½" thick by rolling,
pressing and/or stretching (Figure 51).

Arrange sliced FRUIT PIECES (apple, banana, peach, plum,
pear, apricot, nectarine) down the center third of the
dough (Figure 52).

Spinkle on BROWN SUGAR if you like and your choice of
spices: cinnamon, allspice, nutmeg, mace, anise.

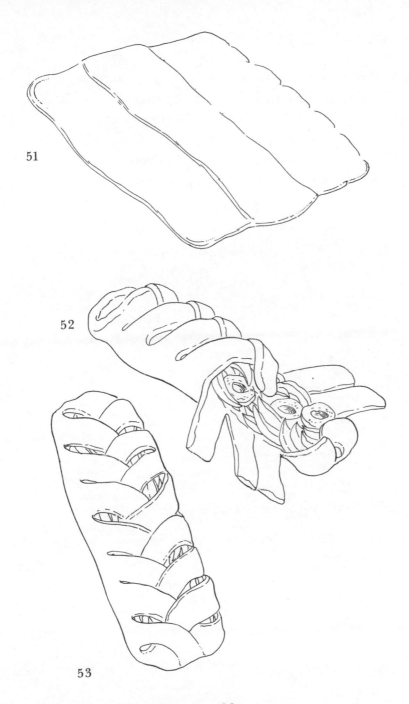

51

52

53

Make DIAGONAL CUTS in the dough about ½" apart from
near the fruit out to the edge.
FOLD the strips alternately over the fruit, stretching and
twisting slightly to form compact loaf (Figure 52).
Place in BAKING PAN or greased baking sheet.
Let RISE 20 minutes.
EGG WASH (and sprinkle with poppy seed).
BAKE 350° for one hour or until golden brown.

Yeasted Bread

YEASTED BREAD

This is the recipe with variations for the bread which pleases almost all of the visitors to Tassajara, Zen Mountain Center. They purchase hundreds of loaves each summer to take home with them. Now you can make it yourself and invent your own variations. There is nothing difficult about this recipe, for there is a wide margin for error, experimentation, and adaptation. Don't give up.

The most delicious food is made by someone who really cares about what they're doing. If you've never made bread, your first batch is going to be better than nothing. After that, no comparison! Each batch is unique and full of your sincere effort. Offer it forth.

43

1 TASSAJARA YEASTED BREAD

The fundamental Tassajara Yeasted Bread recipe.
(Four loaves)

I. 6 c lukewarm water (85—105°)
    2 T yeast (2 packages)
    ½—¾ c sweetening (honey, molasses, brown sugar)
    2 c dry milk (optional)
    7—9 c whole wheat flour (substitute 2 or more cups
        unbleached white flour if desired)

II. 2½ T salt
    ½—1 c oil (or butter, margarine, etc.)
    6—8 c additional whole wheat flour
    2—3 c whole wheat flour (for kneading)

(For detailed explanation of directions, see the GENERAL
DIRECTIONS FOR TASSAJARA YEASTED BREAD,
page 19.)

Dissolve yeast in water.
Stir in sweetening and dry milk.
Stir in whole wheat flour until thick batter is formed.
Beat well with spoon (100 strokes).
Let rise 60 minutes.
Fold in salt and oil.
Fold in additional flour until dough comes away from sides
    of bowl.
Knead on floured board, using more flour as needed to keep
    dough from sticking to board, about 10—15 minutes
    until dough is smooth.
Let rise 50 minutes.
Punch down.
Let rise 40 minutes.

Shape into loaves.

Let rise 20 minutes.

Bake in 350° oven for one hour.

Remove from pans and let cool, or eat right away.

VARIATIONS

Recipes No. 2—16 are examples of possible variations of the Basic Tassajara Yeasted Bread No. 1. *Ingredients are the same as those listed in the basic recipe unless otherwise specified.* All quantities are for four loaves. In each recipe proceed as in Basic Tassajara Yeasted Bread No. 1.

For the Sponge:

Water is partially replaced with eggs, sour cream, buttermilk, or mashed banana in some of the recipes.

Yeast is constant in all but one of the recipes: No. 16 "French" bread.

Sweetening has been specified as honey, molasses, or brown sugar.

Dry milk is constant except where omitted, in the "French" bread No. 16.

The 7—9 cups flour are generally specified as "4 cups white and 4 cups whole wheat", or "use rye flour instead of whole wheat flour", or "use all white flour", etc.

For the second half of the recipe:

Salt is constant.

Oil is constant, unless specified butter, for which melted margarine or oil may be substituted. Oil may be omitted.

For the 6—8 cups whole wheat flour, the following ingredients may be substituted: rye flour, rolled oats, corn meal, millet meal or whole millet, wheat bran, wheat germ, rice flour, barley flour, soya flour. If cooked grains or cereals are added, additional wheat flour will be necessary. Generally only one or two of these grains or flours are added in addition to the wheat flour. If more than three grains (e.g. rye, oats, wheat) are used, the bread tends to lose the distinctiveness of its taste. The use of rice flour, wheat germ, wheat bran and soya flour in particular will tend to make the bread heavy and dense.

Flour for kneading may be whole wheat or unbleached white.

2 RYE-OATMEAL BREAD
Dark, lightened with white flecks of oats, chewy, moist.

I.   *Use molasses for sweetening*
     Use 4 c unbleached white flour, 4 c whole wheat flour

II. *4 c rolled oats*
     4 c rye flour
     Whole wheat to knead

Proceed as explained under Variations, page 45.

3 SESAME WITH CRACKED MILLET
Super-rich, melt-in-your-mouth, greed-arousing.

I.   *Use honey*
     Use 4 c unbleached white flour
     Use 4 c whole wheat flour

II.   6–8 c sesame meal
      2–3 c cracked millet
      4–6 c whole wheat flour

Proceed as explained under Variations, page 45.

4 RYE BREAD WITH SOUR CREAM
Dark, heavy, full rye taste and texture.

I.   Use molasses
      Substitute 2 c sour cream for 2 c water
      Use rye flour instead of whole wheat

II.   4–6 T caraway seeds
      8–10 c rye flour

Proceed according to Variations, page 45.

5 RYE BREAD WITH BUTTERMILK AND WHEAT FLOUR
Rich, eggy taste, lighter than above.

I.   Use molasses
      Substitute 1 c buttermilk and 5 eggs for 2 c water
      Use 6 c unbleached white flour and 4 c rye flour

II.   ½ c melted butter
      8 c rye flour
      4 T caraway seeds
      More white flour as needed

Proceed according to Variations, page 45.

6 SUMMER SWEDISH RYE BREAD
Sweet and scented, light, suitable for sandwiches.

I. Use honey and all unbleached white flour
    Add grated peel from four oranges
    1 T anise seeds
    1 T caraway seeds

II. 8—9 cups rye flour
    Whole wheat flour for kneading

Proceed according to Variations, page 45.

7 CORN MEAL MILLET BREAD
Crunchy, crumbly, sweet, yellow.

I. Use honey
    4 c unbleached white flour
    4 c whole wheat flour

II. 5 c corn meal
    3 c millet meal
    Whole wheat to knead

Proceed according to Variations, page 45.

8 RICE-SOY BREAD
Somewhat heavy, somewhat strange.

I. Use honey
    4 c unbleached white flour
    4 c whole wheat flour

48

II.   *2—3 c roasted* soy flour*
       2—3 c roasted* brown rice flour
       5—8 c whole wheat flour

*to a medium brown; keep stirring over medium flame

Proceed according to Variations, page 45.

9 OATMEAL BREAD
Moist, chewy, sweet taste.

I.   *Use honey or molasses*
      4 c unbleached white flour
      4 c whole wheat flour

II. *5 c rolled oats*
      4—5 c whole wheat flour

Proceed according to Variations, page 45.

10 MILLET BREAD
Deceptively plain taste with sweet crunchiness.

I.   *Use honey*
      4 c unbleached white flour
      4 c whole wheat flour

II. *4 c cracked millet*
      Approximately 6 c whole wheat flour

Proceed according to Variations, page 45.

11 BANANA SANDWICH BREAD
Fruity, light spiced, good for toast and peanut butter sandwiches.

I.   Use honey
     Substitute 4 bananas, mashed, and 4 eggs for 1 c water
     Peel of 4 oranges, grated
     4 T cinnamon
     4 c unbleached white flour
     4 or more c whole wheat flour (until spongy)

II. Whole wheat flour

Proceed according to Variations, page 45.

12 RAISIN BREAD
Surprise.

Add ½ c raisins per loaf to any of the above

13 NUT BREAD
What an interesting discovery.

Add ½ c of any chopped or whole nuts, roasted or
     unroasted, per loaf

14 FRUIT BREAD
What else can you imagine?

Add ½ c per loaf of chopped, soaked or cooked dried
     fruit: apricot, prune, peach, etc.

15 CHEESE BREAD
Toast it for a ready-made grilled cheese sandwich.

I.   *Use brown sugar and all whole wheat flour*

II.   *4 eggs, well beaten*
      6 c grated cheddar cheese
      ½ c melted butter
      Whole wheat flour as required

Proceed according to Variations, page 45.

16 FRENCH BREAD
Crusty old loaves.

I.   *Use double amount of dry yeast*
      Omit dry milk
      Use only ¼ c honey

II.   *Use all wheat flour, whole wheat or unbleached white*

Shape into French loaves following instructions in the Sourdough section (page 87) or shape into plain rolls. Place on baking sheets which have been sprinkled with corn meal. Let rise 20 minutes. Brush with water. Place a pan of water on the bottom of the oven to keep oven and bread moist, prevent drying out. (Refill with water as necessary.) Bake at 425° for 10 minutes. Remove from oven and brush with water. Continue baking at 375° until well-browned, about 15–20 minutes for rolls, about 40–50 minutes for loaves. For added shine, brush tops with garlic butter as soon as removed from oven.

17 TASSAJARA YEASTED BREAD USING WHOLE MILK

A slightly superior loaf.
(2 loaves)
(Use complete recipe page 19 or shorter version page 44.)

I.   ¼ c warm water
       1 T dry yeast
       2½ c scalded milk* (cool to 100°)
       6 T honey or molasses (¼–½ c)
       ¼ c oil
       3½–4 c whole wheat flour

II.   2 T salt
       3½–4 c whole wheat flour or variation

May also use 1¼ c evaporated milk mixed with 1¼ c very hot water—resulting mixture should be lukewarm.

Scald milk by heating to just below the boiling point. Set in cold water for quick cooling. Dissolve yeast in warm water. Add sweetening and oil to cooling milk. When cooled to 100° (not hot, not cold on wrist) mix in dissolved yeast and stir in whole wheat flour until thick, pasty batter is formed. Beat well with spoon (100 times), cover and let rise in warm place 50–60 minutes. Fold in salt and remaining flour as in Tassajara Yeasted Bread recipe.

18 EGG WASH

Beat 1 egg with ¼–½ c cold water or milk. Brush on top surface of bread before baking.

Yeasted

Pastry

YEASTED PASTRY

The yeasted pastry recipes are generally intended for
an occasional, special breakfast treat, or for a picnic dessert.
A little more effort is necessary, a little more time, and
since the reward is perhaps too tempting, this is quite
fortunate.

19 YEASTED BREAKFAST BREAD DOUGH

*This is basically the Tassajara Yeasted Bread recipe with the
addition of eggs. Can be made into various wondrous breakfast delights, as your feeling dictates and your pantry allows:
English muffins, lemon twist bread, Swedish tea ring, prune
filling, date filling, cinnamon roll, pecan nut roll. Make it
on a leisurely Saturday or Sunday morning, or the night
before, and reheat and toast it in the morning. The basic
dough is not so sweet or rich, but generally light. Tradi-
tionally this sort of thing is made entirely with white flour,
but the one called "the best" last year had barley flour and
rolled oats, which added flavor and chewiness to the dough,
along with grainy sweetness.
(The following ingredients will make enough to serve
generously 4—6 people; one loaf.)*

I.   1 c water
      1 T yeast
      2 T honey or molasses
      1/3 c dry milk
      1 egg
      1½ c flour, whole wheat or unbleached white

II.   3 T butter or shortening or oil
       1 t salt
       2—2½ c sifted flour: unbleached white with whole wheat
          for added flavor, or your choice

Proceed as for Tassajara Yeasted Bread (page 19). After kneading and one rising, follow the directions for Swedish Tea Ring No. 20, Cinnamon Roll No. 21, Pecan Nut Roll No. 22, English Muffins No. 23, and/or Lemon Twist Bread No. 24.

20 SWEDISH TEA RING *(see illustrations)*
Looks so good, a blossoming flower of fruit-filled bread.
(Serves 4—6)

Use Yeasted Breakfast Bread Dough recipe No. 19. As dough is rising, simmer until thickened:
       1 c chopped pitted prunes or dates or raisins
       ½ t cinnamon (nutmeg or allspice are good too)
       1 T lemon juice (or orange)
       ¼ c brown sugar (or 1 t vanilla extract)
       1/8 t salt

After dough has risen, roll out to 12" x 14". Spread with fruit mixture (Figure 54). Roll as for jelly roll (Figure 55). Place on greased sheet and join ends (Figure 56). Cut 1" slits with scissors (Figure 57). Twist if you wish (Figures 58 and 59). Allow to rise double in bulk. Brush with egg wash. Bake at 350° for 30—40 minutes until golden brown. Frost with liquidy mixture of beaten egg white sweetened to taste with powdered sugar.

56

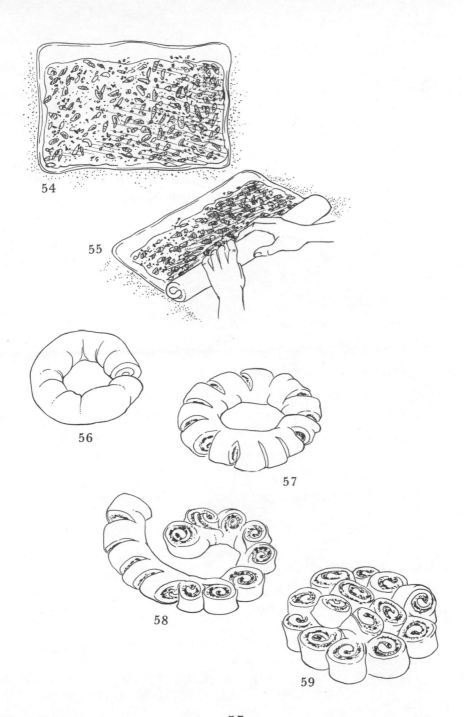

54

55

56

57

58

59

VARIATIONS:

21 CINNAMON ROLLS

What a revelation, making cinnamon rolls for the first time.
(Serves 4—6)

Prepare dough as above in No. 19. Roll out in rectangle about ¼" thick. Brush with melted butter. Sprinkle to taste with brown sugar, cinnamon and raisins. Then roll up, cut in sections, and place flat on greased sheet. Let rise 20 minutes. Brush with egg wash. Bake at 375° for 20 minutes.

22 PECAN NUT ROLL

Another one which captures people before they can say no.
(Serves 4—6)

Prepare cinnamon rolls as above (omitting sugar in filling). Use a pie tin or 9" x 9" x 2" pan. Cover bottom of pan with a thin layer of honey, and sprinkle on ½—1 c of chopped nuts, walnuts, pecans, or others. Place cut rolls next to each other on top of this mixture. Let rise 20—30 minutes. Bake at 350° for 30 minutes. Turn upside down onto serving platter.

23 ENGLISH MUFFINS

A Tassajara summertime favorite which can actually be made
with any yeasted bread dough.
(Serves 4—6)

Follow No. 19 Yeasted Breakfast Bread Dough recipe (page 55). After first rising, punch, let rest 10 minutes. Roll out ¼" thick and cut into 3" rounds or squares. Sprinkle top with corn meal. Cover with dry towel, and let double on board 45 minutes. Bake slowly on ungreased griddle. For each batch have griddle hot at first, then reduce heat to brown slowly, baking 5—6 minutes on each side.

They freeze well.

VARIATIONS:

Use corn meal-millet, or corn-rye recipe (with or without egg), or your choice.

24 LEMON TWIST BREAD
Another old favorite, with tangy, spiced-lemon scent.
(One loaf)

Follow No. 19 Yeasted Breakfast Bread Dough recipe (page 55), adding to the sponge:

½ c raisins
1 T chopped lemon peel
1 t freshly grated nutmeg

Knead, using a minimum of flour, until smooth and satiny. Let rise until double (50 minutes to 1 hour), punch down, and let double again. Divide into as many strands as you would like to braid (2, 3, 4, 6), roll out, and braid, following illustration (pages 60 and 61). Let rise 20—30 minutes. Brush with egg wash. Bake at 350° for 40 minutes. Frost if desired with powdered sugar, grated lemon peel and lemon juice until thick or thin, as you please.

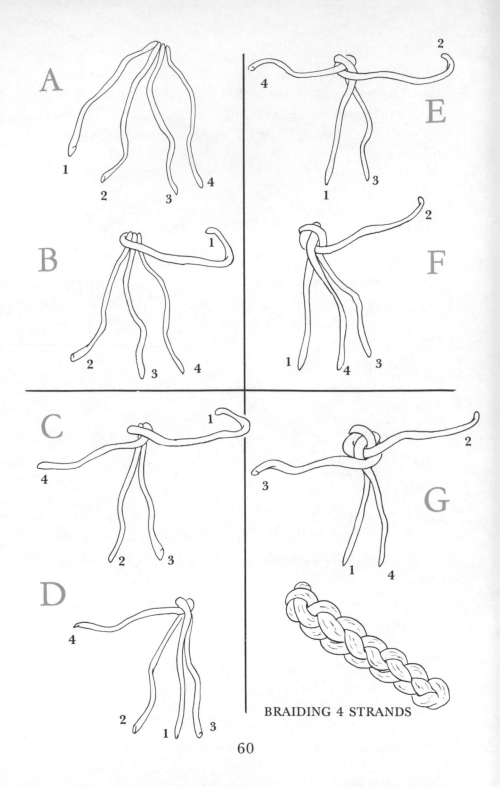

BRAIDING 4 STRANDS

60

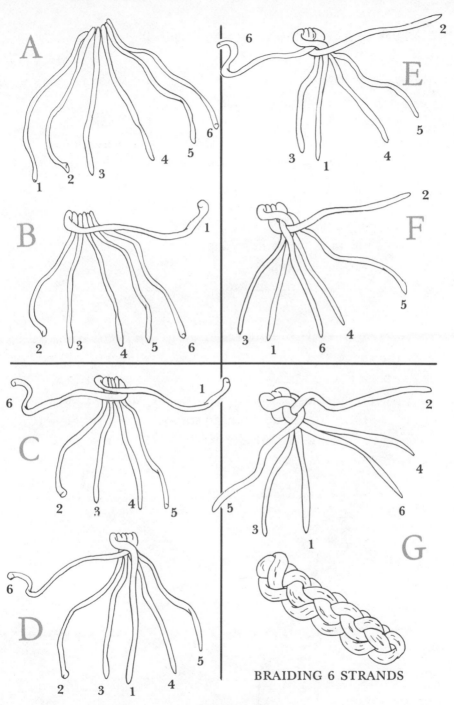

BRAIDING 6 STRANDS

61

25 NORWEGIAN COFFEE CAKE

Very rich.
(Serves 8—10)

> ½—1½ c butter or shortening
> ½—1½ c brown sugar
> 2½ c lukewarm water or 2½ c milk (if using whole
>   milk, scald and cool to lukewarm)
> 2 T yeast
> 2—8 eggs
> 1—2 t salt
> 1 t ground cardamon (lemon or orange peel, citron,
>   raisins optional)
> 11—12 c unbleached white flour with whole wheat
>   added for flavor

Soften yeast in liquid, add about 4 c flour, and a little of the sugar. Beat well, and let rise while creaming butter or shortening. Cream in sugar. Stir in beaten eggs. Add to yeast-sponge along with salt and spices. Add flour as necessary to form soft dough. Knead smooth. Let rise. Pick a shape to form, let rise. Bake at 350—375° in a greased pan for 50—60 minutes.

26 KOLACHES

Sweet ones for picnics and parties; make them as butter-rich, sugar-rich, egg-rich as you like; the final amount of flour will vary accordingly.
(Five dozen)

> 2 T yeast
> 2½ c lukewarm water or 2½ c milk, scalded* and cooled
> 4 c sifted unbleached white flour
> ½–1½ c butter
> 2 t salt
> ½–1 c brown sugar or honey
> 2–8 beaten eggs
> 1 t anise extract, 1 t mace or 1 t nutmet
>   (or ground anise seeds)
> 7–8 c additional white unbleached flour or whole
>   wheat flour

See page 52 for scalding instructions.

Soften yeast in liquid. Add 4 c unbleached white flour and ¼ c brown sugar. Beat well, about 100 times. Cover, and let rise while you cream the butter with the sugar or honey.

Stir in eggs. Fold into risen yeast sponge, along with spice and salt. Fold in additional wheat flour as necessary to form soft dough.

Knead five minutes. Let rise until doubled in volume. Punch down, divide into individual pieces (walnut or egg size), shape into balls, and place on greased cookie sheet. Flatten to ½" height; let rise 20 minutes. Make indentation with your thumb and place filling in it. Let rise 10 minutes. Brush with egg wash, melted butter or oleo. Bake at 350° for 20 minutes, or until golden brown. *(Continued)*

OR, after first rising, roll out dough ¼" thick and cut into squares. Place filling in center of each square, and twist opposite corners together over filling.

KOLACHE TOPPINGS AND FILLINGS

(A) Poppy Seed Topping

> *2 c ground poppy seed*
> *1 c sugar (brown or raw)*
> *½ c honey*
> *1½ c milk*
> *½ t salt*

Mix well, cook slowly for 20 minutes until thick yet spreadable, cool before putting on dough.

(B) Butter Glaze

> *1 c sugar (brown or raw)*
> *½ c unbleached white flour, sifted*
> *1/3 c butter*

Cut butter into sugar and flour and place on top of poppy seed, prune, or apricot fillings just before placing kolaches in oven.

(C) Prune or Apricot Filling

> *2 c cooked, mashed, pitted prunes or apricots*
> *½ c honey*
> *1 T lemon juice*

Mix until ingredients are well blended.

Also: cherry, apple, pineapple, peach or berry filling for kolaches.

(D) Almond Paste

½ lb. ground almonds
Honey to taste
2 eggs, well beaten

Mix eggs and almonds and add honey to taste.

(E) Date Almond Filling

>   ¼ c butter
>   ¼ c honey
>   ¾ c whole pitted dates
>   ¼ c almond paste or chopped almonds

Melt butter and sugar together, stir in remaining ingredients, and cook until thickened.

27 BRAIDED CHRISTMAS BREAD

Like grandmother's been making every Christmas for 50 years.
(2 huge loaves or more smaller ones)

>   ¼ c lukewarm water
>   3 T yeast
>   4 c milk, scalded and cooled
>   ½ c oleomargarine or butter
>   1 c sugar or honey or molasses
>   6 eggs
>   2 T salt
>   1 t mace
>   2 t vanilla
>   1 c raisins
>   1 c walnuts, pecans, or almonds
>   15—18 c wheat flour (with variations as in Basic
>   Tassajara Yeasted Bread)

Mix yeast with ½ c lukewarm water, with a little sugar added. Mix slightly scalded milk and melted oleomargarine and sugar. Add yeast mixture. Add enough flour to make a soft sponge, stirring well with wooden spoon. Set aside. As dough is rising, separate eggs, and beat each part separately. When beating is completed, fold in yolks first, and then fold in (stiff) whites. Let rise until dough is double in size. Then add salt, mace, vanilla, raisins, and nuts. Fold well and start folding in sifted flour. Keep folding in flour until stiff enough to put on floured board. Knead well (150 times) then place in two large bowls and let rise until doubled in size.

Place dough from bowl(s) on floured board in two portions. Lay one aside and cut the other one into nine equal pieces. Roll each piece to a length of 14". Place four lengths together and pinch the ends together at one end. Intertwine them (see illustration braiding of four strands, p. 60), and place this bottom layer on a well-greased cookie sheet. Then roll out three lengths the same way, pinch together at one end, braid and place on top of the bottom layer, which has been slightly greased. Now roll out two lengths and twist together and place on top of second greased layer. PRESS braided lengths together well, since they tend to topple over. Straighten before baking, and check while baking.

Now beat up an extra egg, add a little coolish water and brush top of bread all over. Let rise ½ hour and pre-heat oven to 300° as you make the other half of the dough the same way, placing it on another large cookie sheet. Bake first portion for an hour until well-browned, adding second loaf to oven (if there is room) after it has risen ½ hour.

Unyeasted

Bread

MAKING UNYEASTED BREAD

Unyeasted breads are a basic whole, natural food. As such they have a deep, hearty, honest spirit. Dense and thick crusted, they require a good bread knife for cutting and a certain endurance for chewing. However, they can be made surprisingly light. Generally, this is accomplished by thorough kneading, and lengthy "proofing"* in the pans. So start unyeasted bread the day before you wish to serve it.

Use warm water when mixing up unyeasted breads. Some recipes call for boiling water. This will make a softer dough which is easier to work with. Make the dough slightly moist before kneading on a floured board. The dough can then be more readily kneaded, and an appropriate amount of flour will be incorporated from the bread board. Keep enough flour on the board so that bread does not stick. Scrape up any dough that sticks and re-incorporate it into the mass of the dough.

Follow instructions for kneading given in the general directions (page 26). When kneading is first begun, the dough will tear rather than stretch. Keep working with it until it is smooth and elastic (about 300 kneads). Resting now and then is permitted.

Make into loaves following the directions given for yeasted bread.

When loaves are in the pans, make a wedge-shaped slit the length of each loaf with a knife.

Brush the tops of the loaves with warm water or oil to keep moist. Cover with damp towel and let sit in a warm place for 8 to 12 hours. With some exceptions, as noted.

*Sometimes "proofing" means "rising".

The baking times and temperatures are different for different recipes. If you discover some times and temperatures that work better, please inform the editors.

Bake until sides and bottom are dark brown.

28 TIBETAN BARLEY BREAD

Many people find this to be one of the very best unyeasted breads. (One large loaf)

> 2 c barley flour
> 4 c whole wheat flour
> ½ c millet meal (or roasted sunflower seeds or roasted sesame seeds)
> 1½ t salt
> 2 T sesame oil   ) for flavor and lightness; if no sesame
> 2 T corn oil   ) oil, you can use all corn oil
> 3½ c boiling water

Pan roast barley flour in 1 T sesame oil until darkened. Mix flours together with salt. Add oil, rubbing flour between hands until oily. Add boiling water, using spoon to mix until dough begins to form, then mixing with hands, keeping hands cool by dipping them in bowl of cold water. Mix until earlobe consistency. Knead until smooth. Place in oiled pans. Cut tops lengthwise. Proof 2–6 hours or overnight. Bake at 450° for 20 minutes on middle shelf, then 400° for 40 minutes on top shelf. Crust will be tough but inside tender. If at first you don't succeed, don't be discouraged. Try baking at 350° for 1½ hours.

29 LOS ANGELES UNYEASTED BREAD NO. 1

Deliciously wheaty taste, remarkably high-rising, unsweetened,
with thick crusts and softish insides—it gets across.
(One large loaf)

> *7 c whole wheat flour*
> *1 T salt*
> *Water as needed to make kneadable (3½ c) (warm water*
> *mixes up a little easier)*

Knead 300 times (count them), cover with wet towel
and let sit 12—24 hours in a warm place. Knead 100 times,
put in oiled pans. Cut top lengthwise and let proof 4 hours
in warm place, or 1½—2 hours in 100—150° oven. Bake at
350° for one-half hour, then oven up to 400° for 45—60
minutes.

(The transmitters insist the crust should be *dark* brown,
the bottom black. True, deep, sincere, honest, and, as they
say, pure.)

VARIATIONS: (always use at least 4 c whole wheat flour)

(A) Use 4 c whole wheat flour, 3 c unbleached white flour

(B) Use 4 c whole wheat flour, 3 c rye or barley flour

(C) Use 4 c whole wheat flour, 2 c rye, 1 c corn or millet

(D) You may also substitute buckwheat flour (1½ c is
enough to give it a buckwheat flavor) so use up to
2 c depending on how strong a buckwheat flavor you
want. The rest may be either rye or corn meal or
barley, brown rice, or combination, or all whole wheat.

(E) Use 4 c whole wheat flour, up to 2 c corn meal, millet
meal, rolled oats.

(F) You can add 2—6 T oil per loaf as a variation.

30 LOS ANGELES UNYEASTED BREAD NO. 2

Unleavened, self-rising, using leftover oatmeal and brown rice.
(One large loaf)

> 2 c barley flour or brown rice flour
> 2 c whole wheat flour
> 2 c unbleached white flour
> 1 T salt
> 2—3 c leftover cereals (oatmeal and brown rice, or others)
> (Water)

Roast barley or brown rice flour. Mix with whole wheat flour, white flour and salt. Add leftover cereals.

Mix well. Add warm water a little at a time until of kneading consistency. (Cereals supply moisture, so not much water is needed.) Knead well (300 times). Place dough in bowl, cover with wet towel, let sit 12—16 hours in a warm place. Knead 100 times. Shape into loaf. Place in oiled pan. Slit top. Let rise for 2 hours in briefly warmed oven (350° for 5 minutes), bake at 375° for 30 minutes, then 450° for 30—45 minutes. Sides of loaf should be dark, almost black.

31 UNYEASTED RICHIE II

About which Richie comments, I loved this bread, but it was unpopular. It is quite deep or dark in flavor—appeals to those who like to chew and TASTE the grain. Very satisfying and heavy.
(One large loaf or two small ones)

> 3 c buckwheat flour
> 1½ c cracked millet
> 1½ c bran
> 2 c whole wheat flour
> 1 T salt
> Water to moisten, making pliable

Mix flours, salt. Add water and knead 300 times. Let sit overnight and reknead 100 times. Shape into loaf. Press firmly into pan, slit top, and place in open oven at 200° for one hour. Place pan of hot water in oven, under loaf, to keep oven and bread moist, prevent drying out. (Refill with water as necessary.) Raise temperature to 450° for 30 minutes, then 400° for 20–30 minutes. DARK crust.

32 UNYEASTED RYE OATMEAL BREAD
Dark, with white speckles.
(One large loaf or two smaller ones)

> 4 c whole wheat flour
> 2 c rye flour
> 2 c rolled oats
> 1 T corn oil
> 1 T sesame oil
> 2 t salt
> 3—4 c water, or until doughy-kneadable

Mix flours, rub in oil, mix in salt. Add water gradually, until all flour is moistened. Knead well, 300 times, shape into loaves, cut tops. Proof 2—6 hours, or overnight. Bake at 425° for 30 minutes, then lower oven to 375° and continue baking for 45—60 minutes.

33 UNYEASTED CAROB DATE BREAD
A rich-tasting, fulfilling bread.
(One large loaf or two small ones)

> 5 c whole wheat flour
> 2 c brown rice flour (lightly roasted)
> 1 c buckwheat flour
> ½ c carob powder
> 1 c chopped dates
> 1 t salt
> 4 c warm water

Dissolve carob powder in some of the water. Mix dry ingredients. Mix chopped dates into dry ingredients. Add dissolved carob and remaining water until dough is formed.

Knead dough thoroughly (300 times) on floured board. Shape into loaves. Put in pans. Slit tops. Let stand overnight. Bake at 350° for 1¾ hours. Good served with real butter.

34 UNYEASTED FRUIT AND NUT BREAD

Something of an unyeasted Fruit Cake—a "wholesome" treat.
(One large loaf or two small ones)

> *4 c whole wheat flour*
> *2 c rye flour*
> *1 c roasted barley flour*
> *1 T salt*
> *¼ c oil*
> *1 c raisins*
> *½ c sunflower seeds (roasted)*
> *½ c roasted chopped nuts (not peanuts)*
> *¼ c soaked dried apricots, chopped*
> *3 c (approximately) warm water*

Mix flours, salt. Rub in oil. Mix in nuts, raisins, apricots, seeds. Add water until dough forms. Knead well, 300 times. Put in pan. Slit top. Proof overnight. Bake 1½ hours at 375°.

35 UNKNEADED UNYEASTED BREAD
Never made this, but it must be all right.
(Two moderate-sized loaves)

> 1½ c roasted buckwheat flour
> 3 c whole wheat flour
> 1 c corn meal
> 1½ c brown rice flour (roasted)
> 2—3 T soy sauce
> 1 T sea salt
> 2 T sesame oil
> Warm water, maybe 5 c

Mix all dry ingredients well. Add oil, soy sauce and enough water to form a thick batter (like a slightly soupy cereal). Spoon into oiled baking pans (3¾ x 7½). Bake for 2 hours at 350°. Remove bread from pans and turn upside down in oven until dark brown.

36 UNYEASTED DUTCH RYE BREAD
The heavy soft-chewing moist brick bread pumpernickel I always wanted to make, and finally could after the Dane learned how.
(One large loaf)

> 4 c rye meal (coarsely cracked rye which contains some flour)
> 1 c cracked wheat
> 1½ t salt
> 2 T honey or molasses
> 2 T oil
> ¼ c wheat bran
> 3—3¼ c boiling water
> (Wheat germ)

78

Mix all together. Dough will be wet. Cover and let sit
overnight. Add more bran or wheat flour if necessary in order
to shape loaf. Roll loaf in bran or wheat germ. Bake in
covered pan for 4 hours at 200° with a pan of hot water in
the oven on a lower shelf. (Refill with water as necessary.)
After completely cooled, wrap in moist towel, and refrigerate
for one or two days before serving: with butter, cream
cheese, marmalade, soups, etc.

37 GRUEL BREAD

*Turning leftovers into the staff of life; a "most popular"
bread at Tassajara; has a wonderful high-rise and slightly
sour taste.*
(Per loaf:)

> *4 c rice gruel (cooked-together leftover rice, or other
> grain, soups, vegetables, salad)*
> *6 c whole wheat flour (amount will vary according to
> how moist the gruel is)*
> *1 t salt or soy sauce*
> *¼ c oil (optional)*

Add salt and oil to gruel. Add flour to gruel, first by
stirring, then with hands, until a dough of kneadable
consistency is formed. Mixture should be of "earlobe"
texture, firm yet pliable. Leave slightly moist, as more
flour is added while dough is kneaded on floured board
until smooth (about 300 times). Make into loaf. Place in
oiled bread pan. Brush top with water. Make a ½" deep
cut down the center of the loaf. Cover with damp towel,
and set in warm place overnight. Bake at 350–375° for
75–90 minutes, until sides and bottom are dark brown.

38 ALTERNATE GRUEL BREAD
Heavier than Gruel Bread.

Begin by adding whole wheat flour in an amount equivalent to the amount of gruel. If more flour is required, use rye, buckwheat, or roasted barley flours, corn meal or millet meal, up to 2 c per loaf.

39 LEFTOVER CEREAL BREAD
Kind use for leftover cereal.

Same directions as with gruel bread, using any leftover cereal in place of gruel. May also add chopped nuts, dates, or raisins, ½—1 c per loaf.

40 GRUEL OR CEREAL CRACKERS
Crisp, crunchy

Same directions as with gruel bread. Let dough set in warm place overnight in bowl covered with damp towel (or dough may also be used immediately). Roll dough out about 1/8" thick on floured board. Cut into squares, diamonds, or rounds. Place on greased cookie sheet. Brush with seasoned oil, or garlic butter. Sprinkle with salt and bake in 425° oven for 10 minutes. May also be deep fried or fried.

41 LEFTOVER CEREAL FLATBREAD
Crisp, chewy

> *Leftover cereal*
> *Whole wheat flour*
> *Salt*
> *Water if needed*

Add flour to leftover cereal (oatmeal, brown rice, gruel, corn meal, whatever) until of kneadable consistency. Add salt (about ½ t per cup of flour). Knead well and let sit in bowl covered with wet towel and in a warm place for 4–6 hours, or overnight. Knead again and roll out (about ½" thick) onto oiled cookie sheets. Let rise in warm place covered with damp towel ½ to 2 hours. Brush top with oil, melted butter, or margarine, and sprinkle with salt and oregano, or your choice of garlic powder, minced onion, marjoram, basil, sesame. Bake at 375° for 30 minutes, or until browned all over. Cut into squares, and serve hot.

42 UNYEASTED BROWN RICE BREAD

Even better taste and texture if the rice is sour.
(One loaf)

> *4 c whole wheat flour*
> *4 c brown rice, cooked (or what else you got left)*
> *¼ c oil*
> *1 T salt*
> *Some water, if needed*

Rub flour and rice together between hands to break up rice. Add oil, salt, and water until dough forms. Knead 300 times. Put in oiled bowl and cover. Leave overnight in warm place (slowest oven with door ajar may be all right, or if dried out in morning, remove from bowl, section, and bake on greased sheet 350° for 45—60 minutes—very good). If yet dough, knead 100 times, form loaf, put in pan, slit top, let rise 2 hours. Bake at 350° for 1½ hours.

Sourdough
Bread & Pancakes

SOURDOUGH BREAD AND PANCAKES

Sourdough bread is the easiest bread to make, yet is still very satisfying. Its taste is exquisitely distinctive and exciting. Yummy! Sourdough possibilities include sourdough French, sourdough rye, and sourdough pancakes. Sourdough breads are particularly tasty with bean soups, cheeses, meats, fish.

The making of sourdough bread requires a sourdough starter. Growing in the starter are microorganisms which cause the bread to rise, and give the bread its characteristic sour taste. Mixing the starter with flour and water to a sponge (similar to yeasted bread) and then letting the sponge stand overnight makes the entire mixture sour. (It is now all starter.) The starter should be replenished from this risen sponge before other ingredients are added, and refrigerated in a covered container for the next bread. Fill a jar or crock (not metal) only half full, as the starter will rise some in the refrigerator.

A sourdough starter can be made by combining 1 tablespoon of dry yeast, 2½ cups warm water, 2 teaspoons sugar or honey and 2½ cups flour. Let it ferment for five days, stirring daily. The starter may be kept indefinitely in the refrigerator, although it is perhaps best to use it once a week. If liquid rises to the top during storage, stir it in again. The starter and the sponge are both about the consistency of thick mud.

Another way to make a sourdough starter is: use any sour food, e.g. two-day or older rice, cereal, coconut, fruit, vegetables, milk and mix with some whole wheat flour (2½ cups) and water as necessary to make it spongy. Let it sit 3—4 days, stirring daily, until a distinctly sour smell arises.

85

43 SOURDOUGH BREAD
*Use this same dough for sourdough English muffins,
sourdough cinnamon rolls, etc.*
(Four loaves)

At night:
>9 c whole wheat flour
>1—2 c starter
>7½ c lukewarm water

In morning:
>Replenish starter
>1 c oil
>2 T salt
>10—12 c or more whole wheat flour

Night:

Add starter to flour without mixing. Then mix together
while adding water a few cups at a time, until a thick pasty
batter is formed. Beat well.

Morning:

Remove 1—2 cups from sponge to replenish starter,
and refrigerate for next sourdough bread. Now fold in oil,
salt, and remaining flour gradually with spoon. When dough
comes easily away from bowl, but is still a bit sticky, remove
and place on floured bread board. Knead for five minutes,
adding more flour as necessary. Dough will be a little softer
and stickier than normal yeasted bread. Cut into four
sections and form into loaves. Place in oiled bread pans.
Slit tops. Allow two hours rising in pans. Brush tops with
water. Place in pre-heated 425° oven for 20 minutes.
Brush tops with water again, turn oven down to 375°, and
continue baking for 1—1¼ hours.

44 SOURDOUGH RYE
Delicatessen taste.

Substitute 6—8 cups rye flour for whole wheat flour in morning addition. May be shaped into round loaves and baked on greased sheet, or on baking sheet sprinkled with corn meal.

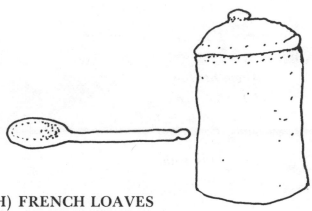

45 (SOURDOUGH) FRENCH LOAVES
How can bread be so good?

May substitute unbleached white flour for whole wheat flour (some or all).

To make French loaves, roll out dough in a rectangle about ¼" thick on a floured board. Starting with a thin end, roll up dough tightly, as you would roll up a carpet.

Pinch seam together and roll about to shape more evenly. Place finished loaf, seam down, on a baking sheet which has been sprinkled with corn meal. Brush loaves with water. Make a ½" deep slit (lengthwise) in the top.

Let rise and bake as for regular sourdough bread loaves.

46 SOURDOUGH PANCAKES
Heavenly.
(2—6 servings)

Night:

Mix up sourdough sponge as for sourdough bread (2½ c whole wheat flour to 2 c water with ½ c starter).

Morning:

Replenish your starter store from this new batch.

For every 2½ c of whole wheat flour used in original sponge, add:

> *1 egg, beaten*
> *2 T oil (corn oil)*
> *¾—1 c milk (whole, canned, or instant)*
> *1 t salt*
> *1 t baking soda*
> *2 T brown sugar*

Mix dough thoroughly with egg, oil, and milk. Combine salt, soda and brown sugar, and sprinkle over batter. Fold in gently. Let sit a few minutes before frying. Make them small.

PANCAKE VARIATIONS:

Add fresh chopped fruit to batter: apples, bananas, peaches, plums, nectarines, apricots.

Add chopped nuts or seeds to batter: sunflower, pine, chopped walnuts, chopped almond, toasted sesame seeds.

Add spices as desired: cinnamon, nutmeg, mace, or coriander.

Pancakes

&

other things

PANCAKES AND OTHER THINGS
TO EAT FOR BREAKFAST, LUNCH OR DINNER
INCLUDING BAGELS

Pancakes are real heartwarmers, especially for Zen monks who have been breakfasting on cereal, beans, and fruit or pickled vegetables. Oftentimes their first stop on the way out of Tassajara is for pancakes with plenty of syrup. More impatient monks, sleepless with desire, have been known to sneak into the still-of-night kitchen and fry up a few yummies (honey, tahini, peanut butter, vanilla, roasted nuts). Generous souls when satiated, they usually tidy up after themselves and leave a couple for the kitchen crew.

No special tricks are involved in making pancakes. Heat your frying pan or griddle until sprinkled water dances around briefly before evaporating. Fry pancakes on first side until small bubbles appear in uncooked surface. Turn (once only) and fry the other side. If center is not cooking, or if browning is spotty or uneven, the pan is too hot.

The other recipes in this section: popovers, cream scones, biscuits, and bagels also can make a heartwarming offering any time of day or night. Coffee cake? As you like it.

91

47 WHOLE WHEAT PANCAKES

Are entirely exceptional, especially served with jam-marbled sour cream and eggs poached with love.
(Serve 6 perhaps)

> 2 c whole wheat (pastry) flour
> 3 t baking powder
> 1 t salt
> 1 T brown sugar or honey
> 3 eggs, separated
> 2 c milk
> ½ c oil

Sift flour with baking powder, salt and sugar. If using honey, add it to the milk and oil. Beat milk and oil into beaten yolks.

Combine yolks, milk and oil with dry ingredients until just blended; then fold in stiffly beaten egg whites. Cook on greased griddle or frying pan. May be made any size.

VARIATIONS:

May be made without separating eggs.

May also be made with fruit puree: apple, apricot, peach, pear, in place of milk or

Add fruit chunks, or

Slip in some tahini, nuts, sesame, or sunflower seeds, or

Use some corn meal or rolled oats, barley flour or buckwheat (½ c).

For waffles use only 1¼ c milk.

48 ORANGE WHOLE WHEAT HOTCAKES

Fragrant, but not as refreshing as plain orange juice.
(Serve 2—6)

> 2 c sifted whole wheat flour
> ½ t baking soda
> ½ t salt
> 2 eggs
> ¼ c oil
> 2 c orange juice, freshly squeezed

Mix eggs and oil and beat. Add dry ingredients alternately with orange juice until well blended. Griddle.

49 O-KONOMI-YAKI

Japanese pancakes made with vegetables (and meat), can be served as midnight meal with warm results. Americans put butter on everything; Japanese prefer soy sauce, but syrup no.
(For about 5 people)

½ cabbage: Chinese, green or red
1 large carrot
½ onion: yellow or purple
3 celery stalks
(½ c meat or fish pieces, if desired, or whatever you have around)
2 c (or more) flour: whole wheat and unbleached white
1 egg, beaten
2 T brown sugar
1 t salt
1 tall can evaporated milk
Enough water to make batter

Chop, shred, dice or thinly slice vegetables and meat. Mix together remaining ingredients to form batter. Fold vegetables into batter and grill. May also be eaten cold on the beach.

50 COTTAGE CHEESE PANCAKES

Creamy, blintz-rich without having to put in filling.
(24 pancakes, light; small to medium)

> 6 eggs
> 6 T flour (whole wheat or unbleached white)
> ¼ t salt
> 2 c cottage cheese (1 big carton)

Separate eggs; beat whites stiff and set aside. Beat yolks with flour, salt and cottage cheese. Fold two mixtures together. Grill, or fry in greased frying pan.

51 POPOVERS

Puffy buns with space for stuffing
(12 popovers)

Mix thoroughly:

> 1 c unbleached white flour
> ½ t salt
> 3 eggs, beaten
> 1 c milk
> 2 T melted butter

Use popover pans or regular muffin tins. Pre-heat oven to 450°. Grease muffin tins and heat in pre-heated oven. When hot, fill 1/3 full with popover batter. Bake at 450° for 20 minutes, then reduce heat to 350° and bake for 10–20 minutes longer. Do not open oven until after 30 minutes of baking or popovers may fall. Eat with butter or jam or cheese.

Popovers may be served for dinner stuffed with meat or vegetables in cream or cheese sauce, with grains or grains and vegetables mixed, or with vegetables (mushroom, parsley, almond) and breadcrumb mixture.

52 CREAM SCONE

*A guest season favorite—has soft velvety texture with a
tangy taste.*
(Serve 4—6)

> 1 c sour* milk (or buttermilk)
> 6 T sugar or honey
> 1 unbeaten egg
> 3½ c flour (unbleached white or half whole wheat)
> 2 heaping t cream of tartar
> 1 heaping t baking soda
> ½ c melted butter or oil

Blend together milk, sugar and egg. Sift in flour with
cream of tartar and soda. Beat well and gradually add melted
butter. Keep the dough moist.

Add up to ½ c more flour as necessary to roll out. Roll
out 1/4—3/8" thick, cut into triangular wedges, dust with
flour. Bake slowly on griddle or in frying pan over medium
low heat so that center will bake (5—7 minutes a side).

VARIATION:
Add ¼—½ c currants or raisins.

*Raw milk will sour much better than pasteurized.

53 FLAKEY BISCUITS

Very rich and tender, also suitable for making cinnamon rolls and shortcake.
(12—16 biscuits)

1 c unbleached white flour
1 c whole wheat flour
½ c butter or margarine
3 t baking powder
½ t salt
2 eggs
½ c milk

Cut butter or margarine into flour, powder, and salt with pastry cutter or two knives, or rub gently between hands until butter or margarine is in mostly pea-sized pieces. Make well in center and add eggs and ½ c milk. Beat eggs and milk with a fork until smoothish. Then continue stirring with fork, gradually incorporating flour, until moistened. Knead dough just enough to bring it together.

Roll dough out on floured board ½" thick. Fold in thirds. Repeat rolling and folding. (The rolling and folding makes a flakier biscuit.) Roll out to ½" thick cut in rounds with cutter or glass. Place on ungreased sheet. Bake at 450—500° for about 8—10 minutes.

For variation add ½ c roasted sesame seeds or roasted sunflower seeds.

54 BUTTER KUCHEN
No kneading, yeasted, tender, moist coffee cake.
(Serves 4—6)

> *1 c milk*
> *1/3 c brown sugar*
> *1 t salt*
> *¼ c shortening*
> *¼ c warm water*
> *1 T yeast*
> *2 eggs*
> *3¼ c unbleached white or whole wheat flour*

Scald milk (see page 52 for scalding directions). Set 1 T sugar aside. Add the rest, with salt and shortening and let cool. Combine water, yeast, 1 T sugar and stir into cooled milk mixture. Beat eggs with ½ cup of the flour. Add to this the remainder of the flour alternately with the milk-yeast mixture, mixing well after each addition.

Pour into 9 x 13" greased pan. Let rise 45 minutes.

Sprinkle on butter topping, made by cutting:

½ c butter into ⅓ c brown sugar and 1 c unbleached
*   white or wholewheat flour*
1 t cinnamon

Bake at 375° for 30 minutes.

55 EGG BAGELS

Best-in-the-west, making 4 dozen bagels and 1 twist bread,
challah; is made with a sponge as in yeasted bread, page 20.

I. 3 c warm water
    1 T yeast
    ½ c sugar
    6 whole eggs, well beaten
    5—6 c unbleached white flour

Beat dough well and let rise. (For onion bagels, add
2 small, diced raw onions to sponge.) After rising fold in:

II. 1 c oil
     1 T salt
     4—5 c whole wheat flour (or unbleached white) until
        dough comes away from sides of bowl

Knead 5 minutes. Let rise 50 minutes. Punch down.
Let rise 20 minutes. Punch down. Cut dough in thirds and
roll into balls. (Cover dough with plastic bag when not in
use to keep a crust from forming and also to keep dough
moister.) Cut one third into 24 pieces and roll out in tubes.
Connect ends of tubes around first two fingers, sealing by
rolling on table. Dip rings into boiling water for 10 seconds
(for that genuine bagel crust). Place on greased cookie
sheet, allowing a little elbow room. Egg-wash and sprinkle
with sesame or poppy seeds, or leave plain. Let rise 20
minutes.

Bake at 425° for 20 minutes. Repeat entire process
with the second portion of the dough.

With the third portion if you want to make a challah,
divide into six portions and braid. (See illustration for

braiding 6 strands, page 61.) Let rise ½ hour, then egg-wash and sprinkle with poppy seeds. Bake at 375° for 50 minutes.

56 WALNUT COFFEE CAKE

Ridiculously too much sugar.
(9" square—serves 4—6)

> 1½ c flour, whole wheat and/or unbleached white
> 2 t baking powder
> ½ t salt
> ¾ c brown sugar
> ¼ c shortening, butter or margarine
> ½ c milk
> 2 unbeaten eggs

Sift flour with baking powder and salt, and blend in sugar. Add shortening and milk and beat 300 strokes. Add eggs and beat 2 minutes.

Topping:
> 2 T melted butter
> ½ c brown sugar
> 1 c walnuts, cut up
> 1 T flour
> 1 t cinnamon

Combine butter and sugar and add walnuts, flour and cinnamon. Mix well.

Spread ½ of batter on bottom of greased pan and cover with ½ of topping mixture. Then repeat.

Bake 350° 30 minutes.

Muffins

&

Quickbreads

MUFFINS AND QUICK BREADS

Muffins have the advantage of being quick and easy
to prepare. Generally they only require about 20 minutes
baking. And people are fond of muffins.

Muffins are made by lightly combining wet ingredients:
egg, milk, oil, honey or molasses with dry ingredients: flour,
baking powder, salt. Mixing just until dry ingredients are
moistened (leaving some lumps) will assure muffins of light,
tender, even texture.

Quickbreads are generally sweeter than muffins, and
intended more for desserts than as part of the meal. Generally
quick breads are baked in loaf pans. Quick breads are done
when a toothpick, chopstick or fork, inserted in the center
of the loaf, comes out dry. Also the bread will have begun
to pull away from the sides of pan and will be springy when
pressed gently in the center of the loaf.

Quick breads may also be baked in muffin tins, making
cupcakes. The baking time is reduced. Muffin batters may
also be baked in bread pans or other baking tins, in which
case the baking time is increased.

57 BARLEY FLOUR MUFFINS

Moist and somewhat heavy, but very tasty.
(12 muffins)

> 2 c barley flour
> 2 t baking powder
> ½ t salt
> ¼ c honey or molasses
> 2 c milk (or water)
> ¼ c oil
> ¼ t vanilla extract

Combine dry ingredients. Combine wet ingredients. Fold dry and wet ingredients together, just until all the flour is moistened. Spoon into oiled muffin tin. Bake 20 minutes at 400°.

58 THREE LAYER CORN BREAD

*Discovered quite by accident; one batter makes three layers.
The corn meal settles. The bran rises. In the middle an
egg-custardy layer. Easy! Glorious! Amazing!
(One 9" x 9" pan serves 4–6)*

> 1 c corn meal (coarse ground works best)
> ½ c whole wheat flour
> ½ c unbleached white flour
> 2 t baking powder
> ½ t salt
> 1 egg
> ¼–½ c honey or molasses
> ¼ c oil
> 3 c milk or buttermilk

Combine dry ingredients. Combine wet ingredients.
Mix together. Mixture will be quite watery. Pour into greased
pan. Bake 50 minutes at 350° or until top is springy when
gently touched.

59 BUCKWHEAT MUFFINS

Not what one expects of a muffin, but fulfilling for buck-wheat lovers.
(Makes 12—16 muffins)

> 2 c buckwheat flour
> 1 T cinnamon
> 1 t salt
> 3 c water
> A sprinkle of brown sesame seeds (roasted)

Mix dry ingredients (except sesame seeds). Add water gradually, mixing thoroughly to make smooth batter. Ladle into oiled muffin tins—½ full. Sprinkle on sesame seeds. Bake 30—40 minutes at 400°. Muffins are crispy outside, soft inside.

60 WHOLE WHEAT MUFFINS

Take your pick, the directions are the same for all of them.
(One dozen large muffins)

> 2 c whole wheat flour
> 2 t baking powder
> ½ t salt
> 1 egg, beaten
> ¼ c oil
> ¼—½ c honey or molasses
> 1½ c milk

Combine dry ingredients. Combine wet ingredients. Fold quickly wet and dry together, just until flour is moistened. Spoon into greased muffin tin. Bake at 400° for about 20 minutes.

61 SOMETHING MISSING MUFFINS

If you are lacking some of the ingredients or desire a plainer food, here are some alternatives. Some are more "muffiny" than others. Generally more rise when sweetened rather than unsweetened, with milk rather than with water, with baking powder rather than without.

VARIATIONS:

(A) Has substance for chewing.
     (One dozen not large but heavy)

     2 c whole wheat flour
     ½ t salt
     2½ c water (or milk)

     Proceed as with No. 60 Whole Wheat Muffins.

(B) Real bite.
     (One dozen pretty hefty muffins)

     2 c whole wheat flour
     ½ t salt
     ¼ c oil
     2¼ c water (or milk)

     Proceed as with No. 60 Whole Wheat Muffins.

(C)   *Surprisingly good rise in this muffin when made with milk.*
(One dozen somewhat tender muffins)

> *2 c whole wheat flour*
> *¾ t salt*
> *¼ c oil*
> *¼ c honey or molasses*
> *2 c water or milk*

Proceed as for No. 60 Whole Wheat Muffins.

(D)   *All that's missing is the egg.*
(One dozen tender muffins)

> *2 c whole wheat flour*
> *¾ t salt*
> *2 t baking powder*
> *¼ c oil*
> *¼ c honey or molasses*
> *2 c water or milk*

Proceed as for No. 60 Whole Wheat Muffins.

62 CORN MUFFINS

Corn muffins are particularly adaptable to seasoning; add a little chile powder, oregano or marjoram.
(One dozen, big, tender and heavy)

> *Substitute 1—1½ c corn meal for equivalent amount of whole wheat flour in No. 60 Whole Wheat Muffins.*

63 BRAN MUFFINS
Wonderful for breakfast, lunch or dinner.
(One dozen large branny muffins)

> Substitute 1 c bran for whole wheat flour. Use ¼ c molasses and add ½ c raisins. Proceed as in No. 60 Whole Wheat Muffins.

64 BUTTERMILK MUFFINS
More tang.
(One dozen large branny muffins)

> Use buttermilk in place of milk. Use 1 t baking powder and ¾ t baking soda. Proceed as in No. 60.

65 FESTIVAL SPICE MUFFINS
Almost a cupcake.
(12 large festive muffins)

Add: ½ t cinnamon
      ½ t mace
      ¼ t nutmeg
      ¼ t allspice
      ¼ t ginger   Proceed as in No. 60.

66 FRUIT JUICE MUFFINS
Different colors!
(One dozen large grey crazy muffins)

> Use fruit juice in place of milk. May omit other sweetening. May add dry milk to fruit juice. (May add food coloring.)

> Proceed as in No. 60.

67 MARMALADE OR JAM MUFFINS
Sweet and sticky
(One dozen large succulent muffins)

Use ½ c marmalade in place of other sweetening.

Proceed as in No. 60.

68 DRIED FRUIT MUFFINS
More chew, more sweet.
(One dozen very large fruity muffins)

Add:	*½ c raisins*
or	*½ c chopped dates*
or	*½ c chopped dried apricot*

Proceed as in No. 60.

69 "ORIENTAL" SPICE MUFFINS
Inscrutable.
(12 large muffins)

Add: ½ t cinnamon
  ½ t cardamon
  ¼ t cloves
  ¼ t nutmeg
  ¼ t ginger

Proceed as in No. 60.

70 NUT OR SEED MUFFINS
More bite.
(One dozen very large muffins)

Add ½ c any of the following:
  Chopped walnuts
  Chopped almonds
  Sunflower seeds (roasted or unroasted)
  Roasted sesame seeds (roast in oven or frying pan)

Proceed as in No. 60.

71 CONFUSION MUFFINS
Watch out!
(One dozen large corny branny granny festive inscrutable oriental fruity succulent muffins)

Combine any or all of the variations.

Proceed as in No. 60.

72 COCONUT CARROT CAKE

Is very special especially if the coconut is sent to you special delivery 3000 miles from New York City.
(Serves 5; use two round cake pans, one 9 x 13 pan, one large loaf pan or two or more smaller loaf pans.)

> 2 c brown sugar
> 1½ c oil (corn or light sesame)
> 4 eggs, beaten
> 2 c whole wheat flour
> 2 t baking powder
> 1 t salt
> 1 T cinnamon
> 1 c chopped pecans or black walnuts
> 1 t flavoring (black walnut or vanilla)
> 1 c grated coconut (freshly grated fresh coconut is
>   incomparable)
> ½—1/3 c grated carrot

Mix sugar with oil and beaten egg. Blend flour with baking powder and salt. Combine dry and wet ingredients. Then fold in cinnamon, nuts, flavoring, coconut and carrot.

Fill greased pans ½ full. Bake one hour at 350°.

73 APPLE NUT LOAF (YEASTED)

Scented with vanilla, zested with orange peel, moist and fruity.
(2 large loaves)

> 2 T yeast
> ½ c sweet cider (lukewarm)
> 1 c honey
> ½ c oil
> 4 beaten eggs
> ½ t salt
> 2 t vanilla extract
> 2 T finely chopped orange peel
> 4 c whole wheat flour
> 4 c raw apples with skins, grated
> 1 c nuts, coarsely chopped (no peanuts)

Optional:
> 1 T cinnamon
> 1 t allspice
> 1 t nutmeg
> ½ c coconut
> ½ c dates or raisins

Soften yeast in cider. Blend honey, oil, eggs, salt and flavorings. Add yeast mixture. Stir in remaining ingredients. Turn into oiled loaf pans. Let rise one hour. Bake at 350–375° for 40–60 minutes.

74 BANANA NUT BREAD

For breakfast or dessert. A heavy.
(1 large loaf)

> 2 c whole wheat flour
> 1 t baking soda
> ½ c oil
> ½ c honey
> 1 grated lemon rind
> 2 beaten eggs
> 2 c ripe banana pulp
> ¼ t salt
> ½ c chopped nuts
> ½ c raisins (optional)

Sift together flour and baking soda. Blend oil, honey and lemon rind until nearly smooth. Beat in eggs. Add sifted ingredients in three parts alternately with banana pulp, beating until smooth after each addition. Fold in chopped nuts. Place in greased loaf pan. bake for 50 minutes at 350° or until fork or toothpick in center comes out dry. Cool five minutes before removing from pan.

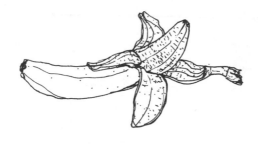

75 DATE NUT BREAD

Whole wheat flour, brown sugar, it's still a rich sweet.
(1 large loaf)

> 2 c whole wheat flour
> 2 t baking powder
> 2 t cinnamon
> ½ t mace
> ½ t salt
> 6 T butter
> ½ c brown sugar
> 2 well beaten eggs
> ½ c milk
> 1 c chopped dates
> ½ c chopped walnuts
> 2 t grated orange rind

Sift together flour, baking powder, spices and salt. Cream butter with sugar and beat in eggs. Add dry ingredients to mixture alternately with milk, beginning and ending with dry ingredients. Fold in dates, nuts and orange rind.

Place in greased loaf pan. Bake at 325° for 60—75 minutes; cool 5 minutes in pan before removing to wire rack. Serve plain, with butter or cream cheese, too.

76 HONEY WALNUT BREAD
Milk and honey—nothing quite like it.
(1 large loaf)

> 1 c milk
> 1 c honey
> ¼ c soft butter
> 2 eggs, beaten
> 2½ c whole wheat or ½ white flour and ½ whole wheat
> 1 t salt
> 1 T baking powder
> ½ c walnuts

Combine milk and honey. Stir over heat until blended. Beat in butter, eggs, flour, salt and baking powder until well blended. Fold in nuts.

Place in greased loaf pan. Bake one hour at 325°; cool 15 minutes in pan. Cool before slicing.

VARIATION:

> Use some or all roasted barley flour. See Tibetan Barley Bread No. 28 (page 72) for roasting instructions. Also can be made without eggs or without baking powder.

Desserts

DESSERTS

LOVE AND KISSES

SWEET DREAMS

A motley collection of recipes, somewhat representative of the wide variety of desserts which may be served. Take your pick. And enjoy yourself.

77 APPLE CRISP

From the days of Tassajara barbecues—tossed salad, half chickens, pork ribs, French bread, baked potatoes, green beans, corn-on-the-cob, red and white wine.
(Serves 6—8)

> *4—6 pippin apples*
> *Juice of one lemon*
> *¾ c brown sugar*
> *1 c whole wheat flour*
> *½ c margarine*
> *Whipped cream*
> *Freshly grated nutmeg*
> *Cinnamon*

Wash, quarter, core and slice apples, thick or thin. Sprinkle with lemon juice and arrange in a greased pan 9 x 13". Mix sugar and flour together. Cut in margarine with pastry cutter until in pea-sized lumps. Sprinkle cinnamon and freshly grated nutmeg on apples. Then sprinkle on flour and sugar topping. Bake for about 45 minutes at 375°. Serve plain, or topped with milk, cream or whipped cream and grated nutmeg. *(over)*

VARIATION:
  Can also be made with peaches, pears, nectarines,
  apricots and persimmons.

78 PEACH KUCHEN
Peach-jewel mosaic set in custard baked with sweet crust.
(Serves 2—12)

  ½ c butter
  2 c flour
  ¼ t baking powder
  ½ t salt
  1 c heavy cream or sour cream
  1 c sugar (brown or raw)
  12 peach halves or 2 packages frozen slices
  2 egg yolks, beaten, or 2 whole eggs
  1 t cinnamon

Cut butter into flour, baking powder, salt, and 2 T
sugar with pastry cutter until it looks like coarse meal.
Press firmly into baking pan. Arrange peaches on surface
to cover. Sprinkle fruit with mixture of cinnamon and
remaining sugar. Bake 15 minutes at 400°. Pour egg yolks
beaten with cream over top, and bake 40 minutes longer
at 375°.

Note: May use other fruits.

79 TORTE WITH SOUR CREAM FRUIT TOPPING

Was the dessert on one of those "best dinner I've had at Tassajara" occasions. A killer.

(Serves 2–12)

½ t mace
1 t vanilla extract
½ c shortening
1 c white sugar
1 c sifted white flour
½ c cornstarch
½ t salt
1½ t baking powder
¼ c milk
2 large beaten eggs

Blend mace and vanilla with shortening. Cream in sugar. Sift together flour, cornstarch, salt and baking powder. Beat eggs and milk together. Add dry ingredients alternately with eggs and milk.

Grease and flour 9" layer-cake pan. Add batter. Bake at 350° for 45 minutes, or until center is dry. Cool in pan 20 minutes, then turn onto wire rack. Turn right side up.

Topping:

Mix a little (2 T) honey or sugar with 1 cup sour cream, along with a little (1 t) vanilla extract. Mix in fruit pieces of the season's choosing.

80 PIE DOUGH

Has taste and lightness, along with workability; use to make any pie or tart.
(One 9" two-crust pie, or two 8–9" one-crust pie, or about 12 tart shells)

> *1 c unbleached white flour*
> *1 c whole wheat flour*
> *2/3 c shortening*
> *¼ t salt*
> *6–8 T ice water*

Sift flours and mix with salt. Cut in shortening with pastry cutter until shortening is mostly pea-sized. Add water and toss with hands, as with salad. Add more water as necessary until dough clings together. Knead lightly and refrigerate one hour, before rolling out.

81 NO-SHORTENING PIE DOUGH

A "cosmic" recipe.
(One 9" two-crust pie, or two 8–9" one-crust pies, or about 12 tart shells)

> *2 c unbleached white flour*
> *½ c oil*
> *½ t salt*
> *½ c water*

While briskly stirring flour and salt with a fork, add oil a small amount at a time. Continue stirring with fork while adding water until dough clings together. Knead lightly. May be rolled out immediately.

126

82 TARTS

To make individual tart shells, which are, in a way, more elegant than a slice of pie.)
(Recipe No. 80 makes 12 tart shells)

Roll pie dough (No. 80 or 81) out on lightly floured board until about 1/8" thick. Cut in about 4½" circles, using an appropriately-sized bowl or can. Place rounds on inverted muffin tin, pleating the dough to fit the inverted muffin cups. To keep the bottom of the tarts flat while baking, place a cookie sheet, pan or muffin tin (right side up) on top of tarts. Bake at 400° about 10 minutes or until nicely browned.

Remove from muffin tin, place right side up and fill with raw or precooked pie filling.

If recipe calls for unbaked pie shell, bake tart shells for five minutes only, before removing from muffin tin. Then place right side up on cookie sheet or baking pan, fill and bake.

Possible fillings include:

> *Meringue pies*
> *Cheesecake*
> *Raw fruit slices mixed with sour cream, vanilla extract*
>   *and honey to taste*
> *Raw fruit slices mixed with mashed bananas sweetened*
>   *to taste*
> *Cooked and mashed dates, raisins, or other dried fruit*
>   *with or without nuts and spices*
> *Fruit mixed with yoghurt and honey*

Garnish with toasted nuts or sesame seeds.

83 CHEESECAKE COOKIES

Quicker than cheesecake and serve more people.
(16 cookies 2" square)

> 1/3 c butter or margarine
> 1/3 c brown sugar
> 1 c whole wheat flour
> ½ c chopped walnuts, or toasted sesame seeds, or
>   roasted sunflower seeds
> ¼ c honey
> 8 oz cream cheese
> 1 egg
> 2 T milk
> 1 T lemon juice
> Grated peel of 1 lemon
> ½ t vanilla extract
> ½ t nutmeg (optional)

Garnish (optional):
Fruit slices: orange, apple, banana, strawberry
chopped nut meats: almonds, walnuts, brazil nuts

Blend together with pastry cutter to make a crumbly texture: whole wheat flour, brown sugar, and butter or margarine. Mix in chopped nuts or seeds. Reserve ½ c for topping. Press remainder into oiled 8" square pan and bake at 350° for 12–15 minutes. Soften cream cheese with mixing spoon. Blend in honey. Blend in remaining ingredients and beat well. Spread over baked crust. Sprinkle reserve crust. Garnish with fruit slices and nut meats. Bake at 350° for 25 minutes. Cool and cut in 2" squares.

Note: If using strawberries for garnish, place on cheesecake after baking.

84 TURKISH COFFEE CAKE COOKIE BAR

Another quick one, try also putting fruit between the two layers.
(Serves 6–12)

 1 c brown sugar
 2 c whole wheat flour
 ½ c butter
 2 T Turkish type coffee, or powdered instant
 2 t cinnamon
 ½ t nutmeg
 Possibly coriander or allspice
 1 c sour cream
 1 t baking soda
 1 egg, beaten
 ½ c chopped nuts

Mix dry ingredients except soda and chopped nuts. Cut in butter with pastry cutter until crumbly. Press half of mixture into pan 9" x 13". Mix remaining half with sour cream, egg, soda, and chopped nuts, and pour on top. Bake at 350° for 20–30 minutes, until springy.

KITCHEN PRICES
Listening to Advice $15.00
Giving Advice $15.00
Arguments $25.00
Hugs and Kisses for free only

85 HONEY BARS

My favorite—they can "age" many months in a tightly-closed tin.
(About 24 large bars)

Have all ingredients ready to mix quickly, before mixture stiffens with cooling.

> 1½ c honey or molasses
> 3 T butter or margarine
> 2 c whole wheat flour
> 1 T baking powder
> 2 T chopped lemon peel
>   or 2 T chopped orange peel
> 2—3 t cinnamon
> ½ t cardamon
> ¼ t cloves
>   Try also mace, allspice, or coriander
> ½ c almonds or other nuts
> ¼ c each of chopped citron and chopped candied
>   orange or chopped lemon peel for variation (optional)
> 1½—2 c more whole wheat flour

Heat honey or molasses in saucepan slowly until liquidy. Melt and add butter or margarine. Sift whole wheat flour and baking powder and add to mixture to make thick batter. Add chopped lemon peel or orange peel, cinnamon, etc. Then add additional flour until dough is somewhat sticky. Pat into greased pans until you have a layer 3/8" thick. Bake about 20—25 minutes at 350°, being careful not to overbake, or cookies will be quite hard.

Remove from pan while still warm. Slice into bars.

86 DATE, FIG OR PRUNE BARS

Whip up in just a few minutes; very sweet.
(One to two dozen)

> 3 eggs
> ½ c brown sugar
> 1 c whole wheat flour
> 1 t baking powder
> 1/8 t salt
> ½ t cloves, ground
> 1 t cinnamon
> ½ t allspice
> 1 t vanilla
> 1 c chopped dates, figs or prunes
> ½ c of broken nut meats

Beat eggs until light. Then gradually blend in brown sugar. Sift together flour, baking powder, salt, cloves, cinnamon, allspice. Add eggs and vanilla and beat until well blended. Add fruit and nut meats. Pour into greased and floured pan 9" x 13" and bake for about 25 minutes at 325°.

87 TOP OF THE WALL COOKIES

This is an original (slightly, anyway) cookie recipe made, baked and eaten the day we put the top of the wall on the kitchen HOORAY! 20 minutes to make 'em, 20 minutes to bake 'em, 20 minutes to eat 'em.
(2 apiece for 50 people)

3 c whole almonds

3 c dates

12 oz semi-sweet
  chocolate bits

8 eggs, beaten

Peel of 2 lemons

5 c whole wheat flour

1 t cinnamon

½ t ginger (optional)

2 c light sesame or corn oil

1 c honey

½ c sesame salt (gomasio)
  or 2 T sea salt

3 c rolled oats

1 c barley flour

½ t cloves

1 t mace

Put almonds in preheating oven (350°). Chop dates and mix with whole wheat flour. Beat oil and honey and eggs together and add to mixture. Stir in chocolate bits, lemon peel, cinnamon, ginger, gomasio (salt), cloves, mace, rolled oats, almonds, and barley flour. Spread on greased cookie sheet. Sprinkle cinnamon on top. Bake for 20 minutes at 350°. Cut rectangles 1½" x 2½".

88 NUTTY GRITTY COOKIES

For using up your old bread crumbs.
(Makes a bunch, obviously)

> 2 c oil
> 2 c honey
> (10 c toasted bread crumbs if you got 'em or 4 c
>   whole wheat flour)
> 6 T salt
> 4 c sesame seeds, roasted (dry roast in pan or oven)
> 4 c sunflower seeds, roasted
> 6 c rolled oats, lightly roasted
> 3 c walnuts, lightly roasted
> 4 c cracked millet
> 4 c corn meal
> 4 c raisins
> 10—12 c water

Blend oil and honey. Add remaining ingredients. Mix well. Add water a little at a time until mixture holds together. Shape (any shape you want) and place on lightly oiled cookie sheets. Bake about 30 minutes at 350°.

89 SESAME CANDY *(Down home halvah)*
You'll need a grinder, a corona handmill, or a mortar and pestle, or a Japanese suribachi, or an electric blender.
(Makes 6—8 moderate, non-greedy servings)

> 2 c unhulled sesame seeds
> 1 T sesame oil (optional)
> ¼ c honey
> 2 T melted butter, margarine, or tahini
> Spices (optional, to taste):
> > 1 t vanilla extract
> > ¼ t cloves
> > ½ t cinnamon
> > ¼ t cardamon or coriander, or nutmeg, or mace

Roast seeds until crunchy, then grind finely. Add remaining ingredients and mix with a spoon and hands. Shape into balls or wafers or press onto cookie sheet and cut.

90 RAW FRUIT CAROB CANDY
Fruit of the earth.
(2 dozen pieces)

> 2 c pitted dates
> 1 c seedless raisins
> Carob powder
> ½ c chopped walnuts (optional)
> ½ c sesame seeds

Grind together dates and raisins. Add walnuts. Add as much carob powder as mixture will hold. Roll into balls. Roll in roasted sesame seeds.

VARIATION:

91 RAW FRUIT CAROB-SESAME CANDY

Mix 1 c sesame seeds (roasted and ground) with the dates and raisins before adding carob powder.

92 SESAME TOFU
Delights, indulges, awakens. A gelatin-like sesame mouth-melter.
(Serves any number, depending on how much you make.)

> 1 part sesame tahini (½ c will make enough for 6—8 people)
> 1 part honey or sugar (or to taste)
> 1 part kuzu arrowroot, arrowroot, or cornstarch
> 5 parts water

Dissolve the cornstarch or arrowroot in part of the water (cold). Mix the remaining ingredients in a thick-bottomed saucepan. Heat gently until all ingredients have dissolved. Then bring to a boil. Pour in dissolved cornstarch while beating with wire whisk or fork. When thickened, lower heat and cook slowly for about 20 minutes while stirring and scraping bottom of pan. Pour into mold or pan, and let cool. Chill if desired.

Note: may be spiced with cinnamon, coriander, nutmeg, etc.

135

93 CREAM CHEESE BALLS

After a fish dinner with a cup of jasmine tea?
(Makes 16—24)

> 1 lb. cream cheese
> ¾ c raisins or chopped dates
> ½ c grated coconut
> 1 T lemon rind or orange rind
> ½ t allspice
> ¾ c chopped almonds, sesame seeds, or sunflower
>   seeds
> (Whole wheat flour)

Soften cream cheese. Mix dates with small amount of whole wheat flour to separate. Mix well all dry ingredients except nuts. Blend in cream cheese. Squeeze everything together in your hands. Shape into 1" diameter balls. Roll in chopped almonds or toasted sesame seeds.

94 ALFA ALFALFA ICE CREAM OR STRAWBERRIES SUZANNE

Take it like you find it, or leave it like it is.

As available:
> *Fruit (juicy) for blending or chunking (how much of*
>   *each is up to you): pineapple chunks, scrumptious*
>   *guava pieces, berries, peaches, nectarines*
> *Cream*
> *Honey*
> *Ice (blender size)*
> *Chopped mint leaves*
> *Lemon—enough to set off the honey*

136

Sample directions:

Blend strawberries and cream and honey to taste. Then blend in ice, or chill thoroughly. Serve in mugs with pineapple chunks or guava pieces, or both, on a hot afternoon.

95 MUSTARD GINGERBREAD

A requested recipe.
(9" x 9" x 2" pan or loaf pan of suitable size)

> *2¼ c sifted whole wheat flour*
> *1½ t baking powder*
> *½ t salt*
> *½ t soda*
> *½ t cloves*
> *1 t powdered mustard*
> *1 t cinnamon*
> *1 t ginger*
> *½ c liquid oil or shortening*
> *1 c unsulphured molasses*
> *1 large egg*
> *1 c hot water*
> *(Whipped cream)*

Sift together flour, baking powder, and salt. Add soda and spices to oil and blend carefully. Beat in molasses and egg. Add flour mixture alternately with hot water. Beat mixture ½ minute and turn into a well-greased and lightly-floured pan. Bake 350° for 45–50 minutes. Cool in pan 10 minutes. Turn onto wire rack, bread board or plate to finish cooling. May be served with whipped cream or fruit sauce.

96 FRESH FRUIT CAKE

No eggs, no baking powder, no sugar, honey or molasses;
just the fresh-fruitiest fruit cake: heavy, yet soft and crumby.
(Two 9" rounds)

> *1 c oil (corn germ oil has best taste)*
> *1 c nut pieces*
> *1 c raisins*
> *1 c coconut*
> *2 c rolled oats*
> *3 c crushed fruit (pulp and juice)*
> *½ t salt*
> *1 t vanilla*
> *2–2½ c whole wheat flour*

Mix all ingredients together to form soft slightly
crumbly dough. Press or spread into greased pans. Bake in
350° oven 40–50 minutes until sides and bottom are golden
brown. Take a peek. Let cool in pan 10 minutes. Turn out
onto plate or board for further cooling. Frost with date
filling and decorate with pieces of fresh fruit.

To make DATE FILLING, place ½ lb pitted dates
in saucepan with water to cover. Simmer 10–15 minutes
until soft. Mash into paste with hand masher, or whip in
blender.

VARIATIONS AND FURTHER INFORMATION:

Use any nuts: walnut, almond, cashew, brazil, hazel or
toasted sunflower seeds.

For crushed fruit, use fresh strawberries, pineapple,
banana, apricot, peaches, nectarines or plums. Apples or

pears may be used if first cooked in water and mashed into sauce, or grated with juice added for liquid.

The amount of flour will vary with moisture content of crushed fruit.

97 HIKERS' MIX

Can be carried on hikes as a light, high-energy food, or mixed into cream cheese as a spread. Hikers' Mix or granola MUST be chewed thoroughly to insure proper digestion.

Roast to taste (separately) (dry roast in frying pan or oven):

3 parts rolled oats	*½ part peanuts*
1 part white or brown rice (washed)	*1 part raisins (please*
1 part sesame seeds	*don't roast the raisins)*
1 part sunflower seeds	

Other possibilities:
>   *1 part almonds (chopped and roasted)*
>   *1 part walnuts (chopped and roasted)*
>   *Pine nuts (roasted)*
>   *Buckwheat groats (well roasted)*
>   *½ part wheat germ*
>   *1 part chopped dates*
>   *1 part chopped dried apricots*
>   *1 part coconut*

Mix together all nuts, seeds and grains, with salt to taste. Cool and add raisins, chopped dates, or chopped dried apricots. Eat now or later, with friends or alone, with honey and milk, with sugar and cream, plain, cooked or raw.

You can eat it dry. You can eat it wet (try it with milk). You can eat it raw. You can cook it. *Don't eat too much because it tends to expand in your system.*

139

98 TASSAJARA GRANOLA

To every 10 c of mixed dry ingredients in No. 97 Hikers' Mix (unroasted—do not use rice), add ½ c oil, ½ c honey, just enough water to moisten all ingredients and aid in mixing in oil and honey. Spread out on cookie sheet or roasting pan. Roast in 250° oven for about an hour or until crunchy brown, stirring occasionally. Add raisins, dates, dried apricot, dried apple or other dried fruit as you choose.

Photograph by Rick Grosse.

ABOUT ED BROWN

Writing about myself: pretty difficult. The whole book is about me, but here goes.

First came to Tassajara when it was still a resort, in May 1966. Got a job as the dishwasher, learned to make bread, soups, and scrub the floor. I could never understand the cooks. One of the cooks quit. Offered his job, I jumped right in over my head. Instantly I understood—in fact I acquired — cook's temperament. What a shock!

During that summer my friend Alan and I did zazen together. One time Suzuki Roshi came down with several students. "The first thing to do in setting up camp is to carry water and gather wood. Now we have carried water and gathered wood," he said.

The next spring I was suddenly head cook of a monastery. Twenty-two years old and about as sure of my position as a leaf which falls in the winter creek. Proceeded to do a lot of things which I didn't know how to do, learning first–hand, the blind leading the blind. Bumped my head quite a bit, and a few other people's heads also. The actual cooking, I discovered, was the easiest part of the job. I was head cook at Tassajara for three summers and two winters, until being completely devoured, bones cast aside, I was finally exhausted of food.

Now I build stone walls, which is really not such heavy work after all.

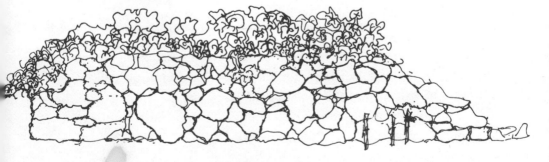

ACKNOWLEDGMENTS

Actually, the fact that this book has come into being is rather incomprehensible and mysterious. In compiling a cookbook to meet the numerous requests of students and guests, I originally chose to complete the project in stages, beginning with breads. Even so, this book has been more than two years in the making. In the meantime I decided to devote myself to working on cooks, rather than cookbooks, and I had rather despaired of seeing this book completed. Fortunately the project has had the help and encouragement of several other people.

I am particularly grateful to Katherine Thanas for her efforts as editor, typist, consultant, proof reader, analyst, friend, and her incorrigible good nature. "What does *this* mean?" she would tease.

I am also indebted to Alan Marlowe for his work as editor, throwing out the rubbish.

Love and thanks to:
Kent and Frances for their beautiful illustrations—the best part of the book.

Diane Di Prima for typing over many of the recipes, running off with the manuscript, and finally returning it.

Peter Schneider for his friendship in supplying advice and editors.

The Zen Center Board of Directors for taking an interest.

Elizabeth Williams for her wonderful encouragement and hospitality: "Get to work."

The Wolfs of Portola Valley for their good humor and persistent prodding, "Please teach."

Judy, Yvonne, Dick and Ginny, and so forth.

Bob and Anna Beck, for getting me started at Tassajara, "teaching me everything I know," as Anna puts it.

For the recipes themselves, I would like to acknowledge and thank the following people: Lynn Good, Loring Palmer, Clarke Mason, Alan Winter, Roovan ben Yuhmin, Sandy Hollister, Kobun Chino, Bill Lane, Bob Shuman, Jeff Sherman, Angie Runyon, Maureen or perhaps Madeleine, Connie, Sandy, Niels Holm, Mary Quagliata, Grandma Dite, and all the other people who have made manifest their love, working in the Fabulous Kitchens of Tassajara.

Lastly, my special thanks and blessings to Jimmy and Ray, my original cooking gurus.

May we all nourish each other.

EDWARD ESPE BROWN
May 30, 1970

ABOUT TASSAJARA

Tassajara is a valley not quite lost in the mountains: natural hot springs, creek, maple, oak, alder, sycamore, and bay, rocks and hills, yucca, sage, and manzanita, quietly changing with the flow of season, now the site of Zen Mountain Center, the first Zen Buddhist monastery in the Americas. Located in Monterey County, California, Tassajara was for many years a resort, a health spa, and an exotic far-out place to imbibe liquor. Zen Center of San Francisco purchased Tassajara in December 1966; what was the bar is now the meditation hall.

Here at the monastery fifty to sixty students, both men and women, practice zazen, the traditional Zen method of sitting meditation, and follow a daily schedule which also includes services and lectures, meals, work, bathing, and sleep. Students eat a comparatively simple diet consisting chiefly of grains, beans, vegetables and fruits. Though lately brown rice is generally served for lunch, in the past bread was served daily, and leftover pieces frequently disappeared at night.

Closed to the public during the winter months so that formal "practice periods" may take place, the Center continues to accommodate guests during the summer months, May through September. Guest food has always been highly complimented, often with the remark, "It's too good. I can't stop eating." Milk, cheese, eggs, occasional meat, and a monkish enthusiasm for good taste make the guest diet more suited to American tastes than brown rice, miso soup, and garden greens. Visitors are delighted that some form of home-made bread is served every meal (accustomed as many have been to "bread" being that pure white, bland,

144

airy, non-substantial filler that comes in plastic, cello, or wax paper). "My, it's good!" they exclaim, and purchase a thousand loaves a summer to take home with them.

Both foods which are primarily part of the guest diet and those which are primarily part of the student diet are included in this book. These recipes arise naturally out of the Tassajara life situation. Isolated, we make our own bread. Working together, we develop many possibilities: food which is earthy, honest, coarse, fulfilling, food which is more refined, soft, soothing, enjoyable. Devoting ourselves, we nourish, satisfy, and please.

Zen Mountain Center's address is Tassajara Springs, Carmel Valley, California 93924.

Tassajara Cooking

by
Edward Espe Brown
Author of *The Tassajara Bread Book*

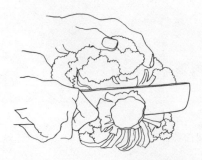

"Handling ingredients thoroughly, openly, gratefully, is an intimate activity, one which provides the basis for nourishment. Ingredients are not limited to food, but include joy, kindness and inspiration, as well as time-consuming effort, mistakes and failures."

Focused on vegetarian cookery, *Tassajara Cooking* examines ways of working with vegetables and other ingredients: grains, beans, dairy products and fruits. Recipes, various cooking methods and cutting techniques are all given. Illustrations are an integral part of the text.

A second section of the book discusses ways of making a wide variety of soups, sauces, salads, and main dishes. "Basic Recipes," which outline the fundamentals of various dishes, are supplemented by specific recipes and variations. Readers are given a framework for exploring, experimenting, discovering; for going beyond written recipes; for "cooking their own cooking."

With additional chapters on knife sharpening, meal planning and kitchen cleaning, *Tassajara Cooking* is a comprehensive handbook.

from
SHAMBHALA